The Lost Art of Good Conversation

The Lost Art of Good Conversation

A Mindful Way to Connect with Others
and Enrich Everyday Life

SAKYONG MIPHAM

HARMONY
BOOKS · NEW YORK

Published in the United States by Harmony Books, an imprint
of the Crown Publishing Group, a division of Penguin Random
House LLC, New York.
crownpublishing.com

Harmony Books is a registered trademark, and the Circle
colophon is a trademark of Penguin Random House LLC.

Some of the slogans used in this book are from *Training the Mind
and Cultivating Loving-Kindness* by Chögyam Trungpa (Boston:
Shambhala Publications, © 1993 by Diana J. Mukpo. Revised
translation of *The Root Texts of the Seven Points of Training the
Mind* by Chekawa Yeshe Dorje © 1993 by Diana J. Mukpo and the
Nālandā Translation Committee).

Library of Congress Cataloging-in-Publication Data
Names: Sakyong Mipham, Rinpoche, 1962– author
Title: The lost art of good conversation / Sakyong Mipham.
Description: New York : Harmony Books, 2017.
Identifiers: LCCN 2017014009 | ISBN 9780451499431 (hc)
Subjects: LCSH: Conversation. | Etiquette. | Oral
    communication—Religious aspects—Buddhism. |
    Conversation—Religious aspects—Buddhism.
Classification: LCC BJ2121 .S25 2017 | DDC 177/.2—dc23
    LC record available at https://lccn.loc.gov/2017014009

ISBN 978-0-451-49943-1
Ebook ISBN 978-0-451-49944-8

Printed in the United States of America

Cover design by Jennifer Carrow
Cover illustration by Rolau Elena/Shutterstock

10 9 8 7 6 5 4 3 2 1

First Edition

To my family

Contents

3.
Be Kind

4.
Enrich Your World

5.
Strive for Conversational Excellence

1

Why Conversation?

Introduction: Bringing Light to a Dark Age

In the eighth century, a great Buddhist master, Padmasambhava, predicted that in the future a dark age would come about. In addition to environmental and social degradation and war, there would be a coarsening of the human consciousness. As a result, good attitude, good conduct, and good speech would wane. Rather than building society around dignified principles of humanity, we would become hardened by opinions and distracted by gadgets, mistaking possessions as a means to happiness when the true sun of happiness shines in our own hearts. Forgetting our basic goodness, we would feel less connection with others as the light of love and compassion dimmed.

In these challenging and chaotic times, I believe that such darkness is now upon us like a long shadow at the end of the day—a diminishing of light. The Shambhala teachings say that this has come about because we are losing our power to determine what to accept and what to reject.

One particular element of our predicament is that our evolving technology intensifies the use of words and images through speed of communication. With the emphasis on speed, the mind is inclined to become more familiar with the language of negativity and develop it further. Because we take less time to think before we speak, we may project our anger around the globe via media before considering the outcome. Once we have uttered our message, karmic consequences are inevitable. The basic laws of the universe have not changed, and we will inevitably suffer as a repercussion of our negative actions.

The great warrior bodhisattva Shantideva said, "Even though we want happiness, out of confusion, we destroy it as if it were our own mortal enemy." At such a time, we must have a plan: a set of principles for how we will act. Without a plan we could easily succumb to the forces of fear and confusion, and our life force would wane.

I have written *The Lost Art of Good Conversation* as a guide to help us bring a little light to the current dark age. The point is to reconnect with the sun of goodness in our hearts and use speech to awaken naturally good qualities in ourselves and others. This approach is based on the path of the warrior, someone who is committed to helping others and who uses everyday life activity to foster awakening. This path is one of joining the spiritual with the worldly. Any activity can be used to change habitual patterns and embody virtue. It all depends on mindfulness, which leads to discernment: knowing what to cultivate and what to discard. Conversation is a perfect vehicle for such practice because it is almost always available.

In the art of conversation we cultivate some sense of goodness, not only in ourselves, but in others as well. When we are gentle with ourselves, we can open our hearts to others. In this book there are guidelines on how to connect with people genuinely, and how not to be swayed by negative emotions. Taking this approach is the gateway to all perfect things. What are perfect things? On a relative level, they are long life, friends, health, and wealth—all the elements everybody is trying to achieve. In addition, they are our enlightened qualities—compassion and wisdom.

In writing this book, I drew my inspiration from my father, the first Sakyong, Chögyam Trungpa Rinpoche, who emerged from the warrior tradition of eastern Tibet with the Shambhala teachings and the message of basic goodness. He did not pull these teachings from thin air but drew on spiritual ancestry dating back to ancient central and southern Asia. He had visions inspired by Padmasambhava and the warrior-king Gesar of Ling; he was also drawing on his own upbringing in Tibet and the teachings he received based on the legendary kingdom of Shambhala—the word means "source of happiness"—which he felt presented themselves at this time as the antidote to our current dark age. On a daily basis, my father would express bits of wisdom, both relative and absolute. These have stayed in my heart, and some I share here. A great deal of this advice is not particularly spiritual. It's just common sense.

Many societies have understood that to grow and be in harmony, we need civility and decency as well as kindness. In modern times, because the ancient wisdom of many cultures has been usurped by materialism and individualism, this civility is often seen as limiting and uncomfortable. Themes such as virtue and dignity are considered outdated. However, as the dark ages become more insidious, people are beginning to realize the value of ordinary human decency. Kindness and respect are as powerful as ever. In fact, they are even more powerful in an age fueled by technology. I invite you to join me in exploring them through the art of conversation.

This book is written in stand-alone chapters so that the reader can reflect on them and practice conversation. The first part of the book explores how to reconnect with the feeling of basic goodness in our lives. The art of conversation depends on this feeling. In the rest of the book I focus on the specific elements of having a conversation. The chapters can be read in the order you like.

Each chapter is accompanied by a reflection. By self-reflecting and practicing good conversation, we can make it our own, as if we had discovered it. This will bring dignity to our daily lives. If enough of us practice this, we will have a huge impact on the future of this planet.

—The Kongma Sakyong II
Jamgön Mipham Rinpoche

What If We Forget How to Have a Conversation?

One day in the grocery store, I noticed long lines at the automated checkout stations, while three cashier lanes nearby were standing empty. I took my groceries to a cashier, a man in his twenties, and asked him why he thought this was happening. Looking over at the line, where several people were checking their phones as they waited, he said, "Most of those people are young. Apparently, people in my generation just don't much like to talk face-to-face." And I thought, *What if we all forget how to have a conversation?*

Now, don't get me wrong. Technology is important; it keeps us all connected in a way, and this book is not about putting down your phone. The danger is that while we are more connected now to the whole world than we ever have been before, we are less connected to people in our everyday life. We're having fewer conversations.

Why is this a problem? We all need someone to talk to. It's easy to become isolated. A conversation is based on physical presence, which is rooted in feeling. All our senses are involved. By talking to someone in person, we gain access to specific senses: appreciation, compassion, and love. These are the feelings that connect human beings to reality, which stimulates our intuition and awareness. If we become conditioned to the computer, then we become one-dimensional. We are less deep as individuals and more shallow, predictable, anxiety-ridden, and irritable. By not having conversations, we're forgetting how to feel.

These days some of us avoid conversation altogether because it requires too much attention. We're accustomed to being distracted and we forget how to focus, so we have trouble listening. We may not have time; we're so busy with school or the responsibilities at work or at home. We may see conversation as a superfluous social gesture. And some of us don't know how to talk to people because we've never been taught.

At the same time, we've become more individualistic and opinionated. Because we want something stable that makes sense in the world, we hold on to themes and ideas that are grounding and meaningful. This fixation creates factionalism and polarity. Identifying strongly with our thoughts and emotions, we mistake them for a solid "me," and then defend that apparition against the world. Social media and the news thrive on these elements. Our digital devices give us a false sense of power, creating a high-tech ego that wants to put its fingers in everything. Yet by having fewer face-to-face conversations, we are simultaneously disempowering the very source that can validate our identity: our relationship with other people.

In addition to being individualistic, our modern society is essentially a society of the anonymous. In earlier times—before the explosion in population over the last one hundred years—not having conversations would have been impossible. Not being polite or acknowledging others would have immediate consequences because we would all know one another. Now it is possible to lead a big part of our lives not knowing anyone, or by ignoring everyone. We care more about ourselves and less about others, and our ability to be civil is breaking down.

Civility is based on putting another person at ease. An opinionated, self-centered, and distracted mind cannot imagine putting another first. As a result, long-established norms of civility, such as respect and tolerance for others' views, appreciation of the truth, and embarrassment about shameful behavior, are in free fall. It seems that fewer people say thank you or please or even hold doors open for others. At the same time, more people are using cell phones in restaurants, and swearing in public is common. There is less consideration for others. It's all about "me." What used to be unacceptable behavior, such as shouting and talking over one another on television or propagating falsehoods, has become commonplace, "normalized," as the standard of social decency erodes.

Losing civility in our daily life, we further lose touch with our capacity to feel. We become genuinely confused about the fabric of reality and social norms, destroying peace within ourselves and others. And before we know it, we're participating in the creation of a world where there's more paranoia and less security for the mind and heart.

This is what is happening in the world today. We are at a dangerous crossroads because when we lose feeling, our exchanges with others lose value. As we gain speed, our relationships become more superficial. As we become more isolated and opinionated, our respect for others decreases. We can't hear them anymore. When this happens, we lose both civility and intimacy. By this, I don't mean romantic love but kindness, the ability to be open and honest with another, to be vulnerable, to be heard.

Life is then defined by the feeling of emotional and social separation—"us" versus "them." We don't really want to interact with others, or we want to interact only with those who agree with us. Maintaining this separation in order to keep out others takes extreme vigilance. This causes stress. It creates fear. We are fighting the natural flow of life.

Great artists use painting, sculpting, or music as their medium for bringing imagination into the world. Likewise, by opening up a conversation with another person, our inspiration has a channel to express itself. It is an art because it transmits feeling. Art brings beauty and meaning into our lives. Beauty is a sense of totality, or wholeness.

It has been said that a dark age is characterized by mass amnesia, in which our consciousness thickens and we forget our art. Then, after a while, we even forget what has been lost. Because language is one of the most subtle and sophisticated aspects of humanity, we must practice the art of good conversation. Simply put, if we don't use it, we will lose it, devolving back into more primal states of being.

From a meditative point of view, the art of conversation is an engagement in mindfulness and, therefore, being present. Mindfulness is the act of noticing. It is not engaging in like or dislike; it is paying attention to being alive. Mindfulness begins with awareness of feeling.

In Hinayana Buddhism, good conversation is right speech: not lying, not slandering, not causing disharmony, not gossiping. In Mahayana Buddhism, it is the open heart and mind that comes from the way we consider how others feel.

From a tantric perspective, good conversation is expressing the mandala principle, where everything is interrelated in a total vision of reality. Just as we are connected to the elements—wind, water, earth, fire—we are inextricably linked to other people.

From the Confucian point of view, good conversation is engaging in social harmony: balancing yin and yang. From the Taoist perspective, it is engaging in the Way, which increases longevity. In terms of civility, it is demonstrating good decorum and manners.

In the warrior tradition of Shambhala, conversation is related to windhorse. *Wind* is the notion of movement, energy, and expanse. *Horse* is the notion of riding that energy. The image of windhorse represents being brave and connecting to the inherent power of life. Good conversation is knowing what to accept and what to reject, and engaging with kindness and compassion, which are the seeds of happiness because they take us beyond ourselves. Rather than categorize these as courtesies or spiritually oriented practices, we can make them center-stage attributes of our lives simply by training our minds in this art.

Our minds are neutral and we can direct them in any way we want. The words we speak come out of our intention. In fact, we are already training our minds all day, every day. However, unintentionally we are training them to get angry, jealous, fearful, and fixated. With these unhealthy emotions, we build a wall of stress that separates us from others. When we are polarized by opinion and hardened by stress, we can't feel.

Ultimately, at the basis, the mind is fundamentally good. *Good* means that there is an opportunity to take the mind beyond the distortion and torment of emotions. We can actually live a life where we are not continually aggravated by negativity, discursiveness, or misunderstandings about how happiness comes about.

It is time to reconnect—to synchronize the mind and heart—in order to find peace, in order to find home, the truth of reality that we have been seeking since the beginning of time. When we know our own goodness, we feel more embodied and ready to engage in an enlightened society, which begins with two people, "just you and me." From the ground of conversation arises the magic of our relationships, enriching everyday life with a built-in sense of enjoyment. A good conversation increases our life-force energy and changes our lives by connecting us heart to heart with another person wherever we may be.

Reflection

With whom do you speak face-to-face? Is your conversational ability keeping up with your technological sophistication? Or is your social conduct becoming more abrasive? Are you losing heart?

The Art in Conversation

When I told my wife that I was writing a book on conversation, she laughed. Even though I do my best as a conversationalist, she is superior by far. In fact, her ability to have a conversation is truly an art and delight, whether it be with a family member or a complete stranger.

After we married, she would enjoy having a conversation while we sat to have tea. As much as I tried to be fully engaged in what was happening, when the conversation meandered, I would sometimes think, *I wonder when she is going to get to the point?* After some time, I came to the realization that not all conversations need a point. Our conversations were not about making a deal, bargaining, or hearing a lecture. Nor was this meaningless chatter. It was a time to be present for each other, an opportunity for everyday intimacy. Talking and listening are essential pieces of a good and healthy relationship. By having this simple time to be together drinking tea—exchanging stories and thoughts and making each other laugh—we were celebrating our special connection. That connectivity is really the heart of all conversations and relationships.

In order to have good conversation, we must appreciate its artistic elements. This art has to do with easing the minds of others, creating valuable and genuine interactions. It is an art of interchange. Through seemingly superficial talk, we reveal our good qualities, and bring about someone else's good qualities. It also indicates control of our emotions when celebrating beauty and grace. It lays the ground for gratitude and respect. It is a warrior practice of kindness using words.

Like the brush on the surface of a canvas, conversation is an image created by words being etched into a mutual consciousness. It is a fluid dance, each word a movement to which the other responds. There is an underlying flow of joy and appreciation as the partners engage in combining words to create a mutually visualized image that can touch the core emotional elements that make us truly human. It engages our minds, our senses, our intelligence, and our imagination. Through conversation we can feel our hearts melt or our eyes water.

Conversation moves from simply communicating

practical bits of information, to celebrating human interconnectedness, to expressing the inexpressible. We can use it to ask questions, which shows our curiosity and intelligence. We can share our knowledge and understanding, our imagination and fantasies. We can also tell stories—colorful descriptions of events that have occurred in our lives or the lives of others. We can use it to deceive—deceiving or misleading others—or we can use it to tell the truth, verbalizing the essence of something. We can explain something in finer detail, further clarifying the truth. We can tell jokes to alleviate stress, pain, and boredom, bringing levity to the situation and expressing insight or a critique. We can use poetic language to express what is ultimately inexpressible, connecting speech and heart.

Each time we speak with someone, there is an **arc** of conversation, which is the journey of an interaction. A conversation can be short and poignant, or long and meandering. In some cases, we know from the beginning how the conversation will play out. Another aspect is the **scope** of the conversation, the breadth—experiences and knowledge it might touch upon—which depends on who we are with and where we are. The scope could be simple and specific, or vast and all-encompassing. The **quality** of the conversation has to do with its depth. An example of shallowness could be a sense of obligation, while a deep conversation would be much more profound. Some may be deeper and purposeful, while others may be lighter and simple. In terms of its **character,** the conversation might be seamless or fragmented. The texture might be smooth or coarse.

A smooth interaction with another has a feeling of synergy—moving from topic to topic with all the ideas being expressed cleanly. A coarse conversation feels bumpy or rough. The connection between ourselves and others feels out of balance. There are interruptions, with many points of contention. But conversations are always changing. A friendship might begin with smooth conversation but, as years pass, become more difficult. Conversely, we could have adversarial conversations with someone that get easier over time.

Even brief moments of conversation can rescue us from being isolated and self-centered. They bring us out and help us engage with the world, connecting with the matrix of human thought. Conversation is a reflection: "I think spring is here." "Oh, yes, the sparrow on my balcony was singing this morning." "Does that mean he's courting?" "Yes, the best song wins the mate." "Really?" It's not necessarily *what* we're talking about, it's *how* we talk about it that affects us. It's about the caring within the words. As we are drawn out of ourselves, we become more other-centered. And this is the key to conversation, to appreciate the one in front of you, which creates a moment of happiness for both.

All the same, some conversations can drag and at times you may find yourself thinking, *Hurry up! Get to the point*. If you're just waiting for the dance to be over, it's not really artful or appreciative. While the other person may be self-centered, the onus falls on you to slow down and remember to be patient. Of course, in certain settings you have to get to the point quickly. If you're driving down the road, for example, you need to know whether to turn left or right. However, even in a short and pointed exchange, there is always the possibility of feeling the pleasure of each other's company. This is artfulness, which comes from our genuine appreciation of the moment.

In ancient Japan, samurai warriors mastered many arts—flower arranging, the tea ceremony, and conversation. They were able to contain their power in the most delicate of activities. A cup of tea conveyed the warmth of perfect friendship, an arrangement of flowers brought the season into a vase. With the same elegance, each warrior could draw a sword and strike a fatal blow, or release an arrow and pierce the heart of an enemy. Such perfect balance and timing in conversation overtakes others before they know it, like the sun moving from morning to midday. The art of conversation is a way to invoke feeling in our hearts and beauty in our world.

Reflection: A Great Conversation

In your mind's eye, return to a great conversation and feel the energy and environment of that moment. What were its qualities? What elements were at play? Spend a few moments feeling the energy of good conversation in your body. Knowing the feeling of good conversation enables us to connect more readily to it.

Words and Breath

Words are the meeting place of thought and physiology. Where they meet is the breath. First, a deep feeling mixed with emotion is bound to a thought and idea. Then these intangible concepts are bound to our being with the breath, an invisible yet physical element that embodies our wind. Wind moves through our vocal cords, tongues, jaws, and mouths to form sounds. These sounds create words that express our mental intentions. *Read this sentence aloud. Do you see what I mean?*

Understanding the relationship between words and breath makes conversation a deep inner experience. We see that our words are not simply hollow verbal expressions leaving our lips. They are the connection between our bodies and our minds. As we utter words with our mouths, our attitudes and our intentions are carried along the breath and vibrate through our bodies. Our thoughts are mixing with our breath into space, where others also experience the words and their vibrations. Like breath itself, words cannot be controlled once they leave our lips. They float along the vapors of time and space like dandelion seeds. There is no predicting where they will land and how they will grow, but they are always affecting the environment, other people, and ourselves.

We can use words and breath for both positive and negative activity. Using them positively is known as a mantra. Using them negatively is known as a klesha. A mantra is an expression of wisdom, while a klesha is an expression of confused emotions. Breath and oxygen are primary elements of health. Whether we are angry, using hard words and hot wind, or peaceful, using soft words and cool wind, how we speak affects our physical well-being.

Speech is a powerful way to affect your own personal karma and that of others. Karma is a truth that anyone can observe: the process of things coming together and having a particular repercussion. When you're not sure of your intention—or don't have one—irrational thoughts, obstacles, and emotions sabotage your mind and vocal cords, and life is difficult. We all experience this every day. For example, you're in a hurry to get to work and snap rudely at the bus driver, and then you're forced to take the next bus.

Thus, every word we utter indicates how fearful or brave we feel. Every word has the potential to lead to peace or war. With the bravery to be present in our lives, we use speech as a way to rise above aggression. Here we define aggression as wanting things to be anything but what they are. When we rise above it in conversation, speech is the warrior's cry of fearlessness.

Words can be a powerful mode of connecting with feelings and thoughts buried within the psyche, a way of releasing and purifying themes that have been stuck in us. In general, we use words to convey the truth. If we express embarrassment or shame about a remark we made to a stranger, or ask for forgiveness for offending a coworker, hidden deceptions are released and unraveled by uttering those words along the winds of our breath. This is the role of confession: it purifies us. Speech has the power to open us in a physical and emotional way. We talk about "opening up" with a friend. Chanting or singing is almost invariably uplifting as we open up with devotion. When we talk about love, we begin to understand more about ourselves as we connect with others.

Even though you can have a depressing or negative conversation, that is not conversation's nature. No matter how it appears, the conversation humanity is always trying to have is about its own worthiness and goodness. Circulating that goodness with words and breath creates energy and therefore wind.

Tantric tradition tells us that the subtle winds within our bodies circulate, and that we breathe twenty-four thousand times a day. This wind represents movement and energy throughout the body. It is associated with life itself. The physical external wind is almost entirely created by the effects of the sun, which every moment showers us with millions of watts of energy. This energy heats the planet's surface, which causes air to rise. Likewise, the wind in our bodies is connected to the sun in our hearts, and through our lives we are capable of creating an infinite amount of warmth by releasing our inherent kindness. Through conversation we circulate the field of power known as windhorse, life-force energy.

Reflection

Sit in a quiet place and begin to count your breath twenty-one times. Then pick a few words or phrases to say. Hear the sound in the room and feel how each word or phrase affects your body. What changes, if any, do you notice in the physical environment? Here are some examples you could say:

- Peace
- War

- It's your fault
- I'm sorry
- Good
- Bad
- Love
- Hate
- Yes
- No
- Thank you

Notice which words you avoid feeling. Can you say them without pulling back? Do you feel genuine in saying words you are comfortable with? To conclude, sit a few moments more. During the day, be aware of any echoes the exercise might have on conversations and things you might say or hear.

Kindness Will Let You Feel Again

The Latin root *conversatio* means "living with; to keep company with, or having dealings with others." Thus we could regard conversation as part of the nature of existence. Language is like a river throughout society, the flow of human connectivity. It is the conduit of openheartedness and inexpressible spirit through which people touch each other. Through conversation we create an endless and fascinating human exchange.

Throughout our lives, we are connected with others—first our parents, then our siblings, friends, teachers, and classmates; then our partner, children, and co-workers. Our identity is a web of interactions. We are so interconnected that our relationships define us. This desire to connect is what we thrive on, and it is also what enables a society to be successful and livable.

Through the Tibetan Buddhist warrior tradition, I

grew up nurtured by the words *compassion* and *fear-lessness*. Although my parents were forced out of their country by catastrophic violence, my father, Chögyam Trungpa, came to the West with the message "If we're going to go forward, there has to be an unequivocal conviction in human goodness." He was a smart man. He said, "People are going to do stupid things, but we cannot let that undermine the integrity of the human race."

Basic goodness for my father at that moment was no different from anyone else's. He was simply opening his eyes and seeing the beauty of the world, and how all situations in life arise from vast openness. This is basic goodness beyond good and bad. It is beauty in the sense of fragility and totality. When we are willing to relax and appreciate that, we feel very open and vulnerable. Vulnerability and heartbrokenness are actually human strengths.

Through openheartedness we are all connected. When we stop and really take the time, we can feel and experience it in any situation in our lives. It manifests in all our positive, negative, and neutral relationships. Even if we hate someone, or hate what that person represents, the heart connection is present: we feel something in relation to that person. Innately we feel for others. The anger, sadness, apathy, or joy that arises in reaction to a friend, an enemy, or a stranger—all of this comes from how our hearts are connected. But our hearts do not discriminate between good and bad. The heart simply feels something.

That ability to feel our world so vividly is what makes us human. This vulnerability demonstrates strength and intelligence because through its energy we are able to contact and perceive our world. It connects us to everything. That connection is invisible but palpable, sparkling, and translucent. Scientists call it limbic resonance, the capacity for sharing deep emotional states with others, which arises from the limbic system of the brain. We have all heard the phrase "Seeing is believing," but truly it's more like *feeling* is believing.

In this way, life is a sensory experience. Engaging our senses is inquisitiveness. Just walking into a room, we can feel the space and the energy, and if we tune in to it with all our senses, we can feel that others are just like us. We are all experiencing the same things—love, hate, heartache, happiness, and sadness. Through this kinship we connect.

Experiencing that interconnectedness in conversation shows us how we feel and how we *are*. If someone does not acknowledge us, we feel hurt and angry. If someone praises us, we might feel happy. Through those feelings, we begin to paint our emotional landscape—seas of love, hills of anger, mountains of frustration, skies of elation, crags of jealousy, sinkholes of resentment, and so forth. In this way, we use emotion to establish our self-identity.

All these emotional states are expressions of the wisdom in our hearts, which innately desires to connect with others. You can see this very clearly in a baby with its mother. However, especially in an age of coarsening values, it is hard to feel our natural kindness because it is often blocked by reactionary emotions. This occurs when we divide the world into us versus them. Then the more we forget our kindness, the more unkindness there is, and the more we forget. This feeds the vicious cycle of a dark age, when many ordinary people cannot feel the warmth of love and compassion that is truly at the center of human existence. Their world is one of too many shades and shadows. Through conversation we can uncover our kindness and illuminate this darkness.

How do we handle emotions? If we recoil from these responses—seeing them as bad, weak, or inherently negative—we are separating ourselves from our own humanity. But if we accept these facets of our totality, we can learn to slow down and look at what's happening. When irritation, hatred, or anger arises, we can ask the question "Where is this emotion taking me?" Ultimately, the heart accommodates all feelings, but relatively, it is up to us to decide what to cultivate and what to discard.

If we can overcome the tendency to fixate on the negative emotion, it is possible to feel kindness again. This is leading life according to windhorse, which runs on virtue. Much of the time we can *feel* what is virtuous because it feels good. It nourishes us. Think of how you feel when you're able to smile at a neighbor even though you've just received bad news. It uplifts your spirits. Now compare that to how you feel when you lose it and yell at your friend. It causes more pain, and brings you down.

Acting out the negativity is a sign that we are pained by our seemingly deficient qualities, absorbed with tightening our self-identity. It is hard to be polite, and communication takes on a depressed or angry tone. Naturally we become defensive and aggressive.

Speech can be reactionary or it can create initiative. This dynamic exists in life, too. Our experience of words is largely based on our communal culture and what realities seem important at the time. At present our society is in danger of creating a reactionary story of fear, hate, and aggression.

I was recently in Chicago working with CeaseFire Illinois and the Interrupters. The topic was how to bring peace. Although there are complicated reasons for the ongoing gang violence there, I began to see that the conflicts really come down to the fact that somebody was not acknowledged. Somebody was not respected. From that lack of kindness there arose pain, anger, and confusion, which then erupted as violence, which increases disillusionment and fear. It may seem like a small thing, but speaking and listening to the people in your daily life can be a way to honor the dignity in one another. When people are kind, a different story is written.

Kindness is empathetic, accepting, and affectionate. It is not as grasping as love or as distant and judgmental as sympathy or charity. It is the emotional sensitivity on which we thrive. When we tap into kindness, we can relax in our being—and then we have the possibility of joining the mundane with the magical. My father called this "joining survival and celebration."

However, when we are unable to feel, we're unable to celebrate. We are afraid of our emotions, which translates into fear of ourselves and others. From this comes the view of "us" versus "them," which is everywhere these days. Because disbelief in human worthiness is so thick, we've reached a point where we must allow ourselves to go through the membrane of this duality and initiate a new story of bravery, love, and compassion, which results in connection and community.

Kindness takes us beyond our own thoughts and feelings to the concerns of others, which enlarges our perspective. A bigger view makes our daily ups and downs look smaller. Kindness allows us to be grateful.

One mind-training slogan of the warriorship tradition says, "Be grateful to everyone." This is challenging advice, because these days, we're much more likely to blame everyone. However, all of our experiences are based on our relationships with others. Without relationships, we cannot develop mindfulness. Without other people, it is difficult to awaken our good qualities. Appreciation takes us beyond blame.

This is not to say that conversation is always easy. Spending time with others can sometimes be unpleasant or jarring. Sometimes we want to retreat. Other times we want to ignore those who are right in front of us. Yet if we want to participate in shifting our story, protecting our planet, and serving others, we have to take part in a nonaggressive way. Nobody has all the answers, but practicing conversation is a way of unblocking dammed rivers and opening up a stream of communal virtue that could lead to freedom from the dark age.

We can do this by having more conversations—genuine dialogues where we are present for each other—and keeping in mind this challenge: Do we have the bravery to be open and vulnerable to the people in our lives? To be kind? Conversation is a daily opportunity.

Reflection

I am a great believer in cause and effect, or karma. By opening our hearts now, we are planting a seed for a future society where "worthy" is the norm. As brave as we have to be to try this, we can aspire to enter every situation with an open mind, which means not rejecting our feelings. Sit down and just feel what you feel now. Accept it without judgment and just be there with it. If you feel good, it is good good. If you feel bad, it is bad good. How can this be? Because we are accepting the totality as it arises from our nature—and our nature is worthy.

Put your hand on your heart if that helps ground you. This is how you can experience the preciousness of life firsthand. Opening our hearts is a socially transformative process through which our pain and confusion can become confidence in human dignity. The result is a sense of peace and contentment that makes it easier to be kind to others.

Windhorse

In the warrior tradition, the mind is considered to be located in the head, the heart, and throughout the body. However, mind and body are ultimately a single entity. This is the feeling of unity, oneness, or centeredness that leads to windhorse. When we have windhorse, we are able to accomplish what we want without many obstacles.

While body, speech, and mind are all important, the mind is the ruler of our lives, and there is a unique relationship between the mind and the breath. When the breath is calm and in control, it is much easier to access the mind and direct our words and actions. However, a heightened thought process such as worry increases the movement of wind. The more erratic the wind, the more it moves throughout the body. We experience it as agitated, discursive thinking and emotional highs and lows, such as panic when you're on a deadline or depression when you think you're going to fail. This agitation translates into stress—blocked energy. Stress is often linked to emotional pressure that we put on ourselves in order to maintain our self-identity in the world.

We attempt to solidify our identity through the two extreme emotions: passion and aggression. These are related to hope and fear. The first tries to embrace; the other tries to repel. With passion, we are trying to draw others in, so there is a seductive element: we like what's happening, and we want more. For example, you're with someone you adore, and everything you say and do is an attempt to entice that person to love you just as much. The root of the word *passion* means "to suffer." With aggression, we don't like what's happening, so we try to make it go away. Waking up in the morning, you feel angry that your sister got the first shower, so you beat on the door and yell. The word *aggression* arises from the Latin, meaning "to attack." Passion and aggression are the forces behind very common emotions we use to try to manage daily life, yet by their very nature they can never be satisfied, because they're rooted in looking outside ourselves for relief.

Passion and aggression often meld into passive aggression, a push-pull style of manipulation or control. The mind-training slogan for this is "Don't act with a twist." We seem to be drawing someone to us, when in truth we're pushing that person away. For example, saying "I'm sorry" to your neighbor when she tells you the music's too loud is a way to mend fences, let go, and move on. But "I'm sorry you feel that way" sounds like you're sorry for something *she* did and that there's something wrong with her feelings. So it's more like an insult than an apology. Conversely, you speak sharply to your brother for eating the last lamb chop, but then you say sweetly, "But I know you really like them." In this style of communication, we're unable to say what's really on our minds, so we deliver a twisted message that cancels itself out.

Passion and aggression stir up the wind and create emotional blockages. Where passion and aggression meet is kindness. In a good conversation, the wind stirred up by these emotions begins to settle down, and the blockages begin to clear. When this happens there is naturally less stress because we are less agitated. Instead of trying to attract, avoid, or manipulate what is happening, with a settled mind it is possible to genuinely feel kindness and speak clearly from the heart.

You can come into contact with kindness by simply paying attention to how you feel now. You will notice that all your sense faculties want to communicate by connecting with the environment. Even when you are alone, there is a wish to communicate. You wish to taste your food and feel the breeze on your face. That very moment of wanting to communicate connects you to all creation, because, just as tentacles do, it extends outward. Stop reading for a moment and tune in to the environment wherever you are. Pay attention to the sounds around you. Do you hear the rain, or perhaps traffic, or the voice of someone on the phone? What do you feel?

Tuning in to where you are settles the wind. Then, from feeling the kindness at your core, you begin to trust yourself. You become more confident in the power of discernment, which leads to more kindness, which increases windhorse. Windhorse represents the joy of freedom in a mind that knows the dangers of using passion and aggression as ways to succeed.

Artfulness in conversation rouses windhorse. When that happens, your speech comes more slowly, but it is more precise. Your sentence structure is good, and what you say has dignity. You are able to find common ground and take a leap. Your speech has a playful quality; it isn't threatening and controlling. Windhorse brings about success by taking you beyond the negativity of twisted emotions, and the result is dignity.

Conversely, allowing discursiveness and distraction to run unchecked weakens windhorse, and we produce our own dark age of obstacles. With a chronically depressed outlook, our wind is not strong. We no longer feel connected and interested in others, which are strong factors in human longevity. Similarly, individuals who are prone to anger can be more susceptible to disease. In addition, there is now clear proof that isolation or poor relationships with others can reduce immunity and decrease longevity. Once interaction is lost, we begin to slowly die. A good conversation means that you are not alone in the universe.

Avoiding passion and aggression may seem impossible. However, there are ways to alleviate isolation, depression, anger, and stress—and conversation is one of them. Honoring your interconnectedness with another increases windhorse, and when you manifest dignity in a conversation, the person you are talking to is more likely to manifest it, too.

We're talking about the intention of accessing our natural empathy and kindness, and how doing this can change our lives. Because there is a direct correlation between personal ethics and our vitality, practicing the art of conversation can create an energetic flow that accomplishes our intentions gloriously while contributing to the ability of the entire society to breathe.

Next time you have a conversation, slow down and pay attention to the words that come out of your mouth. Where are they coming from? What is the intention behind them? What you'll hear is the possibility of something beyond gossiping, complaining, insulting, and disagreeing. There will automatically be lots of gaps in your speech because just by paying attention to it, you'll slow down and talk less. This is a way to interrupt deeply embedded habitual and reactive patterns, and at the same time build confidence.

By strengthening confidence in our own worthiness, we engender confidence in the worthiness of humanity itself.

Reflection

Every encounter is the beginning of a new conversation, even before language is shared. The secret is that we have to be present for it. Before you speak, breathe and find your own spot. What emotions are arising? Can you notice what is happening in your mind and then simply appreciate the space you share with the other person? The conversation has already begun.

Nowness Is the Secret Ingredient

Conversation is a practice of nowness. It is engaging in the power of being on the spot, like a tiger. We are being completely available in the moment with all our faculties engaged.

Through the power of nowness, we are thoroughly living in this moment because there is no other place to be. When it is free from the tug-of-war with past and future, the mind is in a more pliant and flexible state. It experiences levity and relief from stress. There is a quality of neutrality and accommodation. Even though it may be brief, the power of nowness creates a sense of space and openness in our minds and, thus, in any conversation.

If we are present now, there is nothing else. Nowness is complete in itself. It can be transmitted by a look or a smile. A few simple words spoken in this atmosphere can be a powerful exchange. On the other hand, a lengthy exchange without nowness can feel awkward and stressed.

Nowness is often present in conversations marked by intensity. In meeting, in parting, in relating with the ill or dying, the conversation becomes very potent; every word seems larger than life. Our sense faculties and awareness are completely mixed. Everything is present; on a subliminal level, we understand life's preciousness.

When neither individual is willing to touch nowness, the conversation lacks dignity. It becomes habituated and superficial. Questions and answers become rote. Intriguing words become ordinary. With nowness, even ordinary words can be intriguing.

Nowness is related to self-respect. If you're not present with what you say, you're likely not going to say what you mean and mean what you say. Because you can't be authentic, the conversation has no potency. When you don't respect your own words, others don't respect them, either. Conversely, when you respect yourself, you naturally respect others. Nowness is the convergence of these two things. It is simply showing up for your life. There is no other time but now. When two people show up for conversation, it becomes inspiring, interesting, and playful because we can just be there. No one feels as if they have to go somewhere else.

Ultimately, nowness cannot be expressed; it must be experienced. When it is occurring, we know it is occurring, but we can't necessarily locate it. It has a whimsical quality, and yet at the same time, it is completely obvious. That's why nowness is the secret ingredient in good conversation. But we can easily miss it. We make the past into a heavy stone that we ponder, replaying experiences over and over again—what could we have done differently? But the thing about the past is that it's not here now. By the same token, no matter what we think, we have no idea what the future will bring. However, we are planting the seeds for it now.

My father taught me to remember three things in order to maintain nowness:

First, nowness is nonnegotiable. You can't impose what you'd like to be happening onto what is happening now.

Second, nowness requires appreciation, which means being fully present.

Third, you have to be daring and delightful at the same time, which means being free of attachment.

The breath is our vehicle for coming back to the present. It is flowing, never solid, always mixing, never separating. Even the word *now* cannot contain it. This energetic emptiness is, oddly, the only physical anchor we have. Even our heartbeat depends on it. Therefore, the best way to come back to now is to take a deep breath that reunites you with your heart, the center of gravity.

Reflection

Sit still. Be present and notice your surroundings. Try not to be drawn into the past or the future. Enjoy this moment and feel what it's like to be alive.

Exchange Yourself for Others

You can see the power of language and how it connects or separates people when you go to a foreign country. Not speaking the local language creates a sense of isolation: "us" versus "them." If you don't speak the language, it's like having one of your senses blocked. You may be able to see something, but you can't hear or taste it. Conversation connects us to the world in a nearly tactile way.

When we feel connected to others through language and emotion, we discover that "us" and "them" are not so very different. We may have our unique idiosyncrasies, but we discover our similarities as well. The discovery that we are fundamentally the same as everyone else is the Buddhist practice of *lojong*—"training the mind."

Training the mind focuses on exchanging self for other. We use it to access our heart, which knows that others are the same as us and that we are the same as others. We're usually thinking of ourselves, but here we're thinking of others. You put yourself in someone else's shoes. With empathy you imagine what your friend is experiencing and what she must be feeling. You imagine what it is she needs. It opens up your thinking process to take this bigger view.

A traditional Buddhist way of opening up to someone is to remember the kindness other people have shown us. Sometimes this can be very hard to do. We get so fixated on what's wrong in our lives that we forget the positive things that have happened. This instruction begins to loosen us up. Another way of exchanging in this way is to find something delightful about the person—something that draws you in, like the sound of his laugh. Unlike focusing on his shortcomings, this approach opens your heart to him.

This practice of exchanging self for others through conversation leads to a greater and deeper understanding of humanity. It's very basic: we all want happiness, and we do not want to suffer. What would real happiness be? It would be less ego, the lack of struggle, and a fundamental joy and sense of celebration, not only in our own happiness but also in the happiness of others. We would stop trying to guard all our pleasant little situations and open up to the suffering of others.

What stands in the way? Generally speaking, most emotions come out of not clearly understanding the relationship between self and other. When we overemphasize ourselves, pride occurs. In its negative sense, pride is a false sense of confidence. We overestimate our own virtues. Pride naturally stops us from feeling the pain of others because we can't be open to it, and we don't feel genuinely worthy ourselves. But when we overemphasize others, jealousy occurs. When self and other compete, aggression occurs. When self and other become infatuated, desire occurs.

Thus, the way to work with emotions is by constantly engaging in the exchange of self and other. Reversing the tendency to put ourselves first calms the breath, settles the mind, and lets windhorse flow. The more we can put ourselves in another's place, the more harmony ensues. In this light, decorum is not simply social politeness but is a way to gain wisdom and merit.

Doing this practice can vastly expand the mind and open the heart, creating a sense of equanimity, or evenness. You can actually feel the inseparability of all of us. Forgetting that, the mind breaks into us and them, which creates mental and emotional tightness, leading to more anxiety and pain. This is the pain of simply being unable to relax with how things are. Putting yourself in another's shoes, you see life from another point of view.

Exchanging yourself doesn't detract from your own perspective or identity. Rather, the more this exchange opens, the more understanding, love, and compassion arise. Conversation becomes a very powerful way of expanding your horizons, taking you beyond your comfort zone. You feel enriched and healthy, which comes about through connecting with the wisdom of another person. This all comes from being willing to see things from another point of view. When this does not occur, you encourage a fixed point of view. In that case, you use conversation more like a weapon than a flower. It is a matter of the heart being open or closed.

Ultimately, this exchange of self and other leads to the realization that "us" and "them" is simply an illusion. This profound understanding releases our innate love and compassion. These qualities are infinite—without bounds. They flow naturally within the open mind and heart. We can give as much as we wish because the sun of goodness is inexhaustible. You can feel it for yourself when you explore this practice.

Reflection

Instead of the usual aspiration that we all subconsciously make, *"May I be happy,"* bring another person to mind with the thought *"May you be happy."* Thinking of that person, send them this aspiration each time as you exhale. Come back to this practice throughout your day. Simply by taking this bigger view, you will feel a sense of relief and relaxation about yourself and other people.

Decorum

Decorum, or how we behave, is how we relate to others in a polite society. *Politeness* has been defined as "an artificial good nature," but as warriors we would say that somewhat differently: understanding your genuine good nature results in appreciation and politeness. Civil decorum is connected with regarding others as worthy and well, which is connected to having some fundamental faith in your own goodness as a person. Being kind to others is the outflow of this feeling. That is how civil duties—even a simple act like stopping for a red light—reflect the inherent kindness of individuals.

Decorum is related to a sense of ethics—how we manifest and conduct ourselves. For the warrior, decorum is based on gentleness, which involves overcoming aggression, showing strength, and being kind. Gentleness accomplishes all wishes, both worldly and spiritual. It subdues those whose manners are coarse and whose attitude is arrogant or dangerous. When we are gentle, people who are angry and coarse in thought and behavior have no way to respond.

In terms of mental decorum, we apply discernment regarding what we think and feel, and which thoughts to express in conversation. If we think before we speak, then what we say has energy and power because it comes from the foundation of our intention. We are directing and guiding the conversation with forward momentum.

This is different from manipulation stemming from our own agenda. It is us noticing how we feel and thinking about what we are going to say. In doing this, we observe a moment of pause, a second of reflection. Therefore, when the words finally come, they are genuine, and are said with power and sincerity. These are the words we decided to say.

At the heart level, decorum is kindness in its true sense: we are mindful and aware of others and their feelings. In terms of speech, we consider it a general expression of who we are. It is a way to express what we stand for. Every word we utter indicates how fearful or brave we feel.

Conversation is meant to benefit self and others. But in an attempt to benefit, you can bring pain to others, which in turn creates pain for yourself. To understand good decorum of speech, we must understand what virtue is, and in order to understand that, we must thoroughly contemplate it. Reflect on your speech patterns. If you find yourself mostly arguing, whining, insulting, and telling crude jokes, then you are obviously not using good decorum. Virtue has many qualities. In conversation, it is gentleness, lack of aggression, and being kind.

In modern culture, it often seems that everything has to have a point. When this occurs, conversation is no longer delightful. With no joie de vivre, there is no art and no elegance. Just as in meditation, a good conversation is more about the journey than the goal. But it always starts with openness and kindness, which begins in your own heart.

Kindness to yourself easily spills over into relationships with others. However, many of us are blind to our fundamental health and sanity. We're not acquainted with our stream of kindness. We're always giving ourselves a hard time. Having a conversation can compound this because the person you are speaking to is also giving you a hard time. Lashing out is like saying, "I'm unhappy, and I'm going to make you unhappy, too!" This is how a vicious cycle begins.

One mind-training slogan says, "Be friendly to yourself." By slowing down to self-reflect or meditate, you have the opportunity to learn gentleness toward yourself through exploring what is happening in your mind and body right now. When you see harshness, self-criticism, and lack of respect, apply appreciation, mindfulness, and contentment. These qualities are always available. The self-assured strength that grows from knowing we already have what we need makes us gentle. We are gentle because we are no longer desperate.

We might associate gentleness with being demure or afraid. On the contrary, it is lack of aggression. It comes from the insight that being pushy makes things harder. While I engaged in deep study at a monastery in South India, His Holiness Penor Rinpoche, the head of the Nyingma lineage, was very kind and supportive to me, knowing that I held a lot of responsibilities. He always encouraged me to apply gentleness. He would say, "Applying gentleness makes you strong and able to accomplish great things. Aggression makes you vulnerable and only able to accomplish temporary endeavors."

In a short meditation, reflect on your decorum with your sense of self, your emotions, and your moment-by-moment experience. As you begin to self-reflect or meditate, the main thing to keep in mind is that you cannot fail. Any time you spend paying attention, applying the mind to any kind of meditative technique, is helpful. By simply reducing your activities and sitting still, being with yourself, you can learn to let go of the perpetual struggle with your own situation. This is good decorum. As in a good conversation, give space. Offer yourself a little leeway, honesty, and humor. A combination of mindfulness and friendliness is ideal.

Reflection

Reflect on the character of your inner decorum. Do you have discretion in your thought process, or do your thoughts run wild? Are you patient, kind, and loving with yourself? Or are you impatient, judgmental, harsh, constantly taking yourself toward extreme feelings like depression or aggression? How does this inner decorum relate to the decorum you observe in your relationships with others?

2

Be Mindful

Stay Awake

In conversation, mindfulness means being present with your vocabulary, pronunciation, pace, and pitch. You can speak only one word at a time. The words should be enunciated properly, neither too fast nor too slowly, neither too loud nor too soft. When you make the effort to treat the words with respect, their potency makes a lasting impression. Through mindfulness you remember which words you have used. It is related to memory. If you overuse words, your stories and analogies lose the desired effect. Mindfulness also means listening to others, appreciating their word choices, and remembering what they have said.

Laziness is the enemy of mindfulness. It means we aren't motivated to pronounce our words properly or to tell a good story. We can't remember what our friend said. What was the name of that book she recommended? We don't care about the clarity of our communication. Although our halfhearted attempts at conversation may feel adequate, our laziness begins to affect our own energy as well as our reputation. Mindfulness requires effort.

Speediness and excitement can also keep us from being mindful. We are in such a rush that we almost choke on our words. They come out jumbled and we don't really know what we're saying. There is no precision. This is easy to see in our modern mode, where acronyms and half-finished sentences are becoming more the norm. Because we assume people don't have time to listen, we sum things up with unintelligible language. Speed is the result of lifestyle choices we are all making, but it leads to lack of respect for what we're doing. In your conversation, avoid run-on or half-finished sentences, as well as grunting. Let other people finish their sentences and try to listen to what they have to say, for listening is the beginning of slowing down and changing your habitual patterns.

The kind ears of others often make amends for deficiencies in the mindfulness of our speech. However, even with a kind listener, if we're not mindful, the structure of our presentation is always weakened, for mindfulness is the foundation of our words. A speedy culture where there is lack of verbal mindfulness creates an atmosphere of stress for all. Mindfulness of speech reduces stress.

With mindfulness comes awareness, with which we emerge from our habitual self-engrossment into the environment around us. Conversation is an exercise in awareness of ourselves, of another person, and of our relationship with that person. We are observing how we are, how the other person is, and how we are sharing the same space. Keeping the other person in mind, we extend respect and kindness by paying attention. This is known as appropriateness. Our awareness is the judge of what seems appropriate to do or not. In a very simple way, awareness is opening our eyes. When we are paying attention, our decorum is more likely to be appropriate. Without awareness, we are in the dark, not knowing how we are behaving or how someone else is feeling. Half the time we are expressing our thoughts, and the other half we are trying to correct misunderstandings.

In this way, conversation is a continual exercise of awareness. Awareness is the ability to know how we are being. We are self-aware and environmentally aware. We have a sense of how loud we are speaking, whom we are speaking to, and the effect we are having on the other person. It is the ability to tune in to our sensory observations and place ourselves in space.

Without awareness, we are not able to listen, or we are distracted. Therefore, awareness allows us to be sensitive to the situation and the mood. Awareness is the key to good conversation.

A good conversation is not an elocution lesson, but like anything else we master, we first have to learn it slowly. When we are having a conversation with a new person, it is usually best to ease into it rather than blurting everything out. As we become more familiar with another, the pace of the conversation may quicken. In many cultures conversations happen at a rapid pace. This is often due to mindfulness and awareness, the foundational principles of conversation.

Reflection

In any conversation, try using these seven points of mindful speech. What changes do you notice?

- **Listen to yourself**
- **Listen to others**
- **Speak slowly**
- **Speak clearly**
- **Simplify**
- **Appreciate silence as part of speech**
- **Speak from feelings in nowness**

Victory Over War

Frequently, victory is associated with conquering an enemy or laying waste to an opponent. In the art of conversation, victory means overcoming the destructive quality of aggression itself. By rousing windhorse, focusing on the breath and the heart, we are resting in the moment when we first perceive the words someone said, before we react. This moment is actually when and where we can experience the openness from which both warriors and cowards arise.

If we choose warriorship over cowardice, feeling the kindness in our heart, any battle that might arise in a conversation is simply nullified before it begins. By surrendering to our openness, we completely overcome confusion, anger, pride, or any other reaction that might hook us into aggression. To do this, these bad habits should be seen for what they are. Their single purpose is to grow. With aggression, the key is to feel it, not feed it. When you lose your mind, come back. When our words are vindictive, defensive, and cynical, it is because we are uncomfortable with that moment of openness before aggression arose.

However, in every conversation that uncomfortable feeling exists. This isn't because human nature is bad, but because we are simply experiencing something that makes us uncomfortable. Maybe you are shy or the other person is a blowhard. Maybe you don't feel pretty or handsome, or you believe people are focusing on the extra weight you've gained. Maybe you're afraid to express yourself, or feel as if your ideas and feelings will be met with ridicule. The reasons are nearly endless. It takes courage to open up to people and speak.

When we trust ourselves, we're able to relax into that moment, the point when conversations open up and move forward. But unless we can stay with the openness of that discomfort, speed and aggression step in. In that case, we are not victorious; we've been seduced by the enemy and have succumbed to it.

The art of conversation is constant mindfulness of war and peace. When someone says something offensive, we recognize immediately that we're on the razor's edge of how to handle ourselves. *Will I create war or will I create peace?* Often it is not about what the other is saying. It is more that he is trying to destabilize us with his words. Can we be strong, not lose our confidence, not fall into the trap of a word game? Can we see what is happening and conquer our own anger? By doing this, we disarm the aggression arising in others.

In these intense scenarios, a variety of approaches are needed, as one solution may not work. First, space is your friend. Breathe. Slow down. Don't talk for a while. This defuses the conversation while you deal with your anger. But in order to resolve it, you have to find a way of looking inward to deconstruct or release your anger.

Consider the futility of anger and its destructive power, for example. Has it ever really solved a problem for you? Try bringing your mind from your head down into your heart. How does it feel? Tell yourself it's okay to lose this argument, or it's okay to be wrong. As we become more proficient at releasing our anger, we develop the skill to just let it go.

Every disagreement is essentially the same argument, again and again. Therefore, when dealing with anger and other strong emotions, you are not only trying to resolve that one argument, but also attempting to shift your habits. As the mind-training slogan says, "Change your attitude but remain natural." We usually have the attitude of protecting our own territory. The advice here is to change that attitude by thinking of the other person first. Applying humor is another way to shift your habitual pattern. When both parties in a disagreement are being silly and childish, they bring levity into the situation.

Good conversation rides the edge of peace and war, aggression and confidence. If we are not aware, aggression can roll in and blanket us like a fog. If we remember the sun in our hearts and let it shine, we can maintain our peace.

Reflection

When you feel people getting angry at you, empathize with them before you react to the anger. This will take great control on your part, but it will help bring peace and equanimity to a situation. Try to see the cause of their emotion. Are they hurt by something you said? Perhaps they are just having a bad day. Whatever it is, first put yourself in their shoes and *then* respond to them. Make the connection. Engage in peace.

Discipline Brings Joy

Joy and happiness are often confused with having fun; we think doing or saying whatever occurs to us is enjoyable. In reality, joy and happiness often come from having discipline. In general, having a positive, generous, and engaged attitude leads to feeling satisfied and content. Conversely, selfish, tight, and negative thoughts make us feel sad and insecure. Thus, how we handle these thoughts directly influences our ability to have a conversation. If we can't determine which thoughts are appropriate to express, we can easily hurt others' feelings or damage our reputation. Because poor relations with others cause grief, our enjoyment decreases. In this way, good conversation is integrally mixed with good mental discipline.

I read a fascinating study about the influence of negative and positive elements of conversation, and how negative behaviors have a stronger impact. It showed that when we face or express negativities like criticism, rejection, or fear in conversation, our bodies produce higher levels of cortisol, the stress hormone that shuts down the thinking center of our brains and activates fight-or-flight behaviors. This also happens when we try to convince others about our opinions or when they try to convince us. We become defensive, reactive, and sensitive. It takes twenty-six hours for our bodies to process that reaction—plenty of time to etch the negative encounter on our memories.

On the other hand, facing or expressing positive behaviors such as active listening, expressing concern, dreaming of a successful future together, inviting discussion, or being open to a difficult conversation brings an increase of the feel-good hormone oxytocin. By activating networks in our prefrontal cortex, this hormone elevates our ability to communicate, collaborate, and trust others. However, oxytocin metabolizes more quickly than cortisol, and its effects are less dramatic and long lasting.

The fact that negative encounters have a greater impact than positive ones, with longer-lasting results, is a strong motivation to increase our awareness of how our conversational behavior affects ourselves and others. What if we were to double up on these positive behaviors? Mindfulness and awareness give us the ability to choose words that are truthful, show concern, and demonstrate that we are open to hearing others' opinions—all skills that build connection and trust. We're bound to make mistakes sometimes, and it's easy to get caught up in a mood. However, even aspiring to apply discipline in our speech benefits others, and we can learn from our mistakes.

In some conversations secrets are exchanged. Those should be respected. If you're told a secret and you tell someone else, you have violated the trust and intimacy of your friendship, not to mention your own sense of discipline.

Especially in a dark age, sometimes people think that keeping secrets can only mean we are concealing some form of negativity. But it is sometimes good and necessary to keep a secret. For one, some inner aspects of our lives should never be shared. Also, when we reveal secrets to inappropriate people, it is like divulging things to children that they are too young to understand. Not only do the parents lose credibility and dignity, but the information can also inflate children's egos and self-righteousness, and we set them up for disappointment.

On another note, in terms of words you've exchanged, even if you've disagreed, saying negative things to others about your partner does not help anyone, and shows a lack of discipline.

Also, if there's something about yourself you'd rather no one else know, the only way to guarantee that you will get your wish is to have the discipline not to tell even one other person. We trust others not to misuse what we have said, but we never really know how a particular word will be received.

In terms of developing discipline, physically it is helpful to reduce all activities and be still by meditating for even ten minutes a day. Through meditation you learn to notice when you are lost in thought. When you have a thought—no matter how wild or bizarre it may be—you label it "thinking" and come back to the breath, to the physical situation. That's the mental discipline. Then the verbal discipline is that while you're doing this, you're conscious of the space and the silence, even though at times it can seem quite noisy due to what suddenly sounds like a waterfall of thoughts.

In a conversation, sometimes all varieties of thoughts and emotions come into your mind and you are simply overwhelmed. You might even blame your partner for your emotional state. In such a case, the best practice is to close your mouth and look at your thoughts. If you consider who is responsible for the thoughts in your mind, eventually you realize that they are not coming from the other person. You are creating those emotions yourself, and often they are coloring your mind so strongly that you are projecting them onto the other person. For example, you might accuse someone else of lying when it is you who are lying. You imagine your friend is angry at you when, in truth, you are mad at her—or perhaps at yourself. On the other hand, you might project that others feel as fabulous as you are feeling. In any case, you cannot apply discipline unless you see your habitual patterns. It is much easier to see your habitual tendencies if you practice meditation regularly.

Reflection

Are you discerning about what you say? Contemplate the effects of unbridled and thoughtless statements you have made in the past and how they have affected yourself and others. Contemplate how other people's thoughtless words have made you feel.

Now think about how positive statements make you feel and how you can uplift others.

Meditate

When we practice meditation, we strip away the words and come to an inexpressible experience of our own being that happens only when we let ourselves relax, feel who we are, and be there for it. That's a very important moment because when we feel who we are in our hearts, then no matter what experience we are having, we are staying with the confidence of goodness. We are learning a path of nonattachment. Relatively, we have a lot of experiences, but ultimately we see that there really is no good day or bad day if we are thoroughly there for it. This is not a belief, but a feeling that we become familiar with and embody by practicing meditation for a while each day.

Meditation begins with taking an upright posture: open in the front, straight in the back. This position allows us to rest in our own vulnerability and strength.

However, if we don't allow ourselves to connect with the quality of feeling, this is harder to access, so the first step is to allow ourselves just to feel. In feeling, there is a sense of unknowing and knowing. Instead of relating to it as a minor sensation, connect to your sense of feeling as a sign that you are alive.

As you meditate, maintain mindfulness of the body and its language, which is the breath, as well as awareness of how you're holding your mind, which is feeling and emotion. By labeling thoughts and following the breath, you engrain the experience of letting thoughts go. Don't judge the thoughts as good or bad; just notice when you're thinking and return to the breath. Equanimity toward what is happening engenders a quality of steadiness, and at the same time frees you to continually move forward out of your comfort zone and into the open space of possibility.

Meditation trains us in the skills of mindfulness and awareness. Mindfulness is remembering what to accept and what to reject. Awareness is the act of seeing whether one is engaged in mindfulness or not. It is the self-awareness to remember what to accept and what to reject, and to do it. If we do not apply mindfulness and awareness, then our thoughts and actions go to the lower realms. Like animals, we engage in life without vision. If one simply has mindfulness but no awareness, one cannot practice and progress in daily life. One has no staying power and therefore cannot accomplish anything. Also, one cannot be aware without being mindful. Thus, mindfulness and awareness are companions in conversation, and we can develop them through meditation.

Reflection

Commit yourself to a ten-minute-daily meditation practice. How does it affect your body, your speech, your mind? At the end of a week, do you notice any differences in your relationships with others?

Greater Intention Brings Greater Joy

Consider your intention. The intention by which you begin a conversation can have a dramatic effect on the outcome of your exchange. How you come to your intention can take time if you are preparing for an important conversation, or it can be more immediate if you run into a friend on the street. Either way, all conversations arise from some intention.

Therefore, intention serves an important role in the arc of a conversation. We can begin a conversation with an attitude of openness and kindness, or with a feeling of tightness and animosity. The words we express in conversation are simply an extension of our intention.

Generally, intention comes with a sliding scale. It begins with a narrow scope. In the most limited range, conversation focuses on ourselves—our own thoughts, worries, and ideas. The next level of intention includes the other person—her ideas, thoughts, and emotions. A greater intention includes all those around us.

For example, we may be out to dinner, having a conversation. The first level would be to engage in the conversation only when it is something we are interested in, which normally focuses on ourselves. The next level is conversing with the people sitting next to us, even if we are not interested. The last level is engaging with everyone at the table with a sense of openness. Naturally, the greater the intention, the greater sense of openness is required.

In our modern life, conversation can become truncated and speedy when our intention is limited and self-centered. In this case, it becomes a challenge to have expansive and open conversations. Being in a rigid state of mind limits the parameters of talk, which leads to a tight, restrained conversation. You become emotionally and verbally stingy. You have trouble giving compliments and listening to other points of view. Naturally, if you are pessimistic about the potential of the conversation, or if you're not interested in the other person, the conversation will take on that character of tightness.

If you are in a more generous state of mind, your intention is more expanded. It is more open and playful. The greater the intention, the more delight and enjoyment will come about.

It is always helpful to have a period during the day when you feel expansive—whether you're dining, having a drink with a friend, or sitting down for coffee or tea. Having a sense of magnanimity brings warmth to the heart and leads to stronger friendships and a deeper quality of life.

Reflection

Examine your intentions for the day when you wake up in the morning. If your intention is tight—stressed, focused on yourself—then your experiences and conversations will be tight, with a speedy, perfunctory feeling. If your intention is open—relaxed, focused on others—then your conversations will be versatile and enriching throughout the day.

Experiment with this.

Riding the Energy of Conversation Brings Vitality

When two people are present and engaged, there is a natural rapport, and an egoless exchange occurs. The energy of windhorse arises out of mutual respect for each other and the conversation. When there is no genuineness or truth being exchanged, someone has become self-serving and is being deceptive. At that point, we might say that the energy of the conversation has become hot air.

The energy of conversation depends on myriad factors—time, place, and the character of the individuals—but whether the conversation is short or long, there is always that element of energy. The communal campfire is fueled by the genuine intention of each of us as well as the words we utter. Even though the energy cannot be seen, it nourishes the health and well-being of the participants. Even when we're feeling down and depleted, a brief genuine exchange can invigorate us.

When both individuals ride the energy of the conversation, it stays with us even after we've parted. For example, a spirited discussion with friends about Beethoven's quintets can enrich our listening pleasure for weeks. By engaging in words and ideas that have the tenor and purpose of enhancing a situation, the energy held in those ideas is unleashed, and people's spirits are uplifted.

In the most basic way, the flow of windhorse, especially in conversation, relates to whether the exchange is truthful or deceptive. Manipulative or complicated schemes quickly dampen any energy. Because certain individuals may be fixated on their own troubles, they habitually try to nullify the energy of conversations. This ultimately compounds their own unhappiness, and at the cost of others' social grace. For conversations to go well, especially in a social setting, it is best to be simple and genuine.

When the exchange is based on truth, there is naturally a forward momentum and windhorse is released. When the exchange is based on deception, there is a reversal in momentum. One or both people are covering their tracks. Without trust, naturally there is a tension, a knot of stress that blocks windhorse. It may be intense but it is not forward moving. Instead of uplifting us, the conversation becomes mired in paranoia and suspicion. Similarly, if two nations trust each other and engage in conversation—another name for diplomacy—trade ensues, and this exchange revitalizes both. But if nations do not trust each other, no treaties are signed and there is economic stagnation. We experience communication breakdown. The energy of the conversation is a clear determinant of how things are going. If we can trust each other in conversation, we are able to relax and open up. There is a natural exchange of feelings, emotions, thoughts, and ideas, which creates energy.

Obviously, we have varying degrees of relationships and trust. We may be able to be truthful about certain things and need to keep other things hidden. The balance will depend on life's realities and our relationships. All these elements are felt within the flow of the conversation. The relation between truth, deception, and windhorse is based not on morality as such, but on the dynamic and intention between people. Bringing freshness and flexibility into conversation, we maintain energy through the continuum of our day and life.

However, a conversation where you're carrying the lion's share of the emotional weight can be depleting. The other person may not respond, or there may be awkward pauses and everything feels clumsy. Or you may bear the brunt of another's bad mood or his lack of self-control. Naturally, you must moderate your own energy in relation to these kinds of conversations. This could mean taking space to reflect, putting yourself in another's shoes, or simply leaving the room. If this happens frequently with the same person, ask yourself: *Is this what I want to be talking about? Is this the person I should be talking to?*

On the other hand, in having conversations with those of deep learning or wisdom, we might feel very blessed. Speaking with upright individuals with virtuous lifestyles can inspire us to follow their example. Even in conversations with children, their purity and simplicity can provide a welcome respite. People just being in a good mood can enhance our spirits. Exchanging with others and connecting with their energy affects our own energy, and thus we need to be aware of these dynamics.

Reflection

In the morning, reflect on your energy. What is its quality? How much do you have? Think about how you would like to use that energy throughout your day to connect with others. After your day, reflect on how you used your energy. When did the energy feel free-flowing? When did it feel depleted, stagnant, or stale?

3

Be Kind

Leap In with Bravery

Beginning a conversation is an act of bravery. When you initiate a conversation, you fearlessly step into the unknown. Will the other person respond favorably or unfavorably? Will it be a friendly or hostile exchange? There is a feeling of being on the edge. That nanosecond of space and unknowing can be intimidating. It shows your vulnerability. You don't know what is going to happen. You feel quite exposed. There's a chance you'll experience embarrassment. Yet this very feeling is what allows you to connect to the other person.

Feeling vulnerable is an act of gentleness. Bravery is an act of fearlessness. Without these two, conversation will never be initiated. Vulnerability is feeling, and bravery is staying with that feeling. Through those two elements, you dare to exchange yourself with others. Not only are you able to put yourself in their shoes, you are such a daring person that you can take a leap.

Therefore, starting a conversation has the quality of leaping. Without bravery, you may never ask someone out on a date. You may never invite someone to dinner. You'll miss out on meeting people who could become friends.

Bravery is different from being aggressive, foolish, or just hoping for the best. Aggression forces itself on a situation. It comes from a place of anger and insecurity. Bravery comes from being synchronized—in the moment, mindful and aware of your surroundings. Then you leap. When you say, "Hello," "How are you?," or "Good day," there is an atmosphere of magnanimity. In that moment you are expressing your state of being. Similarly, conversation can be a form of celebration. You are happy to be alive, and happy that the other person is alive, too.

The act of beginning a conversation is a very revealing moment. Do you cower from the situation? Or are you ready to leap? By leaping, you are deciding to connect to your own heart, which is expressed by saying, "Hello."

Reflection

Think about whom you would like to connect with and visualize yourself saying, "Hello." Imagine tapping into the power that is generated by that first interaction.

Acknowledge and Initiate

Conversation becomes an art when it transports us from self-absorption to being aware of the thoughts and feelings of others. Thus, the first element of conversation is being aware of others.

All languages have a greeting: *Hello, Bonjour, Namaste, Ni hao, Hola, Tashi delek*. With these words, a line of communication has been opened. Even if we do not have much in common, that initial acknowledgment can be felt as a bond. Its importance lies within our own language as well.

Conversely, by not acknowledging others, we are intentionally or unintentionally dismissing their existence. Those who are not acknowledged feel insecure, angry, and possibly vindictive. This can lead to misunderstanding, hurt feelings, discord, and even war.

When we walk up to the checkout counter at the convenience store, we may not even acknowledge the person working the register. We just hand her our credit card without making eye contact or saying hello. In our modern world, this has become the norm. If we do say, "Hello," the person might be surprised that we are acknowledging her existence. This lack of courtesy affects our society as a whole. Thus, simply saying hello is a meaningful and mindful endeavor.

In English, when we say, "How are you?," the most important word is *you*. We are turning our attention to another. The word *attention* can mean "to be drawn out." We are drawn out from the self-absorption of ourselves to notice the existence of another, which is the notion of *how*. Two human beings are acknowledging each other. That moment is important for the species and the planet.

In Chinese, there is a greeting that means "Have you eaten?," which shows concern for others. In Tibetan, when we greet someone we say, *"Tashi delek!"* *Tashi* means "auspicious." *Delek* means "joyful." We are saying, "I hope everything is auspicious and joyful for you." This greeting is intended to uplift and enrich another's life. When meeting another person, we greet him with our good intention. We are celebrating his life and his existence. It is a little bit like saying, "Happy New Year!"

This initial contact of acknowledging and confirming each other's existence does not have to involve confirming each other's egos. The art lies in the interchange. We are slowing down, acknowledging the moment. Rousing windhorse, we take a leap. In offering our confidence to the other person, there is delight in being alive.

Having made the initial acknowledgment and remembering where we are, then it is up to us to decide how the conversation will proceed. Generally speaking, it is best to start with experiences that are immediately available to both people. Begin with the weather or a detail about what's in front of you now. Ultimately, you and your conversation partner share what it is to be human. With that perspective, sharing little things is easy.

Reflection

Before entering into a conversation, or even greeting someone at work or on the street, find something you respect about the person you are about to engage. You don't even have to tell him about it. Just notice how your respect changes the way you speak to him.

Find Common Ground

There are many circumstances in which you may find yourself with the opportunity or social obligation to start a conversation with someone you don't know. If you are starting from apparently no knowledge of the other person, at least you know that you share the situation you are both in. Some good conversation openers might be, "How do you know James and Sharon?" (The party hosts.) "Are you visiting San Francisco, or going home?" (On an airplane.) "Is this your first visit to the Shambhala Center? How did you find us?"

When initiating a conversation with a stranger, avoid asking overly personal questions. If you lead by asking someone if she's married or what his job is, you may seem to be prying. However, if the other person volunteers that she has recently changed jobs or he is having trouble with his health, that may be okay as a topic. Likewise, launching into your own personal situation too readily might make the other person feel awkward.

WITH SOMEONE YOU KNOW

No matter what your relationship, be attentive and kind regarding the other's feelings. Most people like to be appreciated. Showing interest is hospitality; it invites them in. Enthusiastic words at the appropriate time will often move the conversation forward. For example, after greeting someone, we might say, "What a splendid speech you gave!" or "Your garden is looking so beautiful this spring." Depending on the mood and the person we're talking to, the conversation can then be directed in a variety of ways. Whether brief or meandering, the dance has begun.

If you believe conversation to be an irrelevant nicety, it is likely to feel like a shallow attempt at interchange. This is known as "small talk," as opposed to "big talk," which indicates that there is seemingly more important subject matter. It is true—there is. But each kind of dialogue has its place, and all conversation is important. If you feel that small dialogue is beneath you or demeaning, you come across as arrogant or insensitive, as if you don't care much about what others think or feel. And when you habitually disdain the shallower end of the conversational spectrum, others *do* feel uncomfortable sharing deeper thoughts and feelings.

WITH SOMEONE WHO DOES NOT SHARE YOUR VIEW

When conversing with someone you don't agree with, find simple common ground to build connectivity and friendship. Instead of focusing on where you disagree, build on a variety of subjects that can strengthen the relationship, such as a cuisine or a sport you both enjoy. Common ground provides a pathway of communication, which leads to trust. At meetings or business gatherings, try talking about food, drink, going for a walk, playing golf, or going for a run—all these activities allow for common experience. Then we find ourselves conversing with others. By doing this we build connectivity and trust.

Through trust, friendship can be established, and then more difficult subjects can come up because we experience a sense of freedom that allows us to be true and authentic. We also understand better, empathetically, how another perceives things. We begin to see that not all their views are wrong and not all our views are right. We learn to let go. Through appreciation of each other, we are willing to compromise. Previous problems can then be approached because we have more tools to work with.

In negotiations, it is good to find small things to build on. Ultimately, if there are root differences we know are difficult to bridge, both parties must be willing to live with the fact that we may not agree on all things. This is a natural part of the reality of living in the world with other people.

Reflection

Reflect on your skills in building connections and developing trust. How flexible are you when you don't know someone or she disagrees with you? Are you able to compromise, accept the results, and let go? Or do you measure the result against your expectations?

RESERVED OR OUTGOING?

Some people are introverted and some are extroverted. If you are more reserved, you may have to put extra effort into conversation. Shyness often arises from fear of making a mistake, feeling exposed, or lack of conversation skills or confidence. Often we are so wrapped up in our own emotions that we're unable to feel others' state of being. It takes determination and practice to come out of your shell, but there are ways to do it.

Stay caught up on current events and always have a topic in mind as an opener—preferably nothing to do with politics. Or notice something about the other person; it could be the color she's wearing or her name. Then take the leap and begin a conversation. "That's such a beautiful color. It reminds me of the ocean in Bermuda. Have you ever been there?" Or "'Driskill,' you say? Any relation to the folks who own the hotel?"

The more conversations you begin, the more confident you will feel. Learn to flash on your own presence first, however that makes sense to you. For example, you can take a breath, or feel the place where your feet meet the floor. Then place your awareness on the other person. It also helps to have a favorite all-purpose opener to get things rolling. A friend of mine says, "How's your heart?" He claims that asking this question—and making a commitment to really listen to the answer—has made for some extraordinary conversations.

If you are extroverted, you may need to practice toning it down. Again, the advice is to be present, forget about yourself, and feel the state of others. Keep in mind that people may not be interested in hearing your advice, the details of your life, or your pet peeves. They might not think your children are so adorable. They might like to get in a word edgewise. The power of silence is a friend to the extrovert, but the person who doesn't speak at all might arouse suspicion. At the same time, shy people can be good conversationalists and outgoing people can be challenged by a simple conversation.

Reflection

Think about someone in your daily life you don't normally pay attention to and decide to acknowledge him the next time you see him and to be attentive to his response. You could decide to say, "Hello, how are you?" to the person who's always reading the newspaper in the lobby of your apartment building. Make a sincere attempt to engage. Through this simple practice, you can make some wonderful connections.

Choose the Right Time and Place

As a young man, every summer I would accompany my father to a meditation retreat in the Rocky Mountains. There would be several hundred people attending these retreats. We would all stay in tents on the side of the mountain. One of our favorite tents was a large Tibetan tent decorated with the classic motif of tigers and lions, reminding us of the rich nomadic culture we come from. In the evenings, we would sit around the fire. Being outdoors with the fresh air, seeing the stars, and staring into the burning embers of the fire that would crackle and hiss was a warm and precious environment. The heat from the fire created a sense of intimacy.

Within this setting my father and I would have intimate conversations. He might tell me the story of his escape from Tibet or what his wishes were for me. In turn I would tell him what was on my mind and in my heart. This environment was so powerful that it played equally into the conversations and was as important as our words and expressions. There is something very primal about two human beings expressing themselves next to a fire. The notion of campfire, warmth, and hearth is now held in our modern kitchens. The stove, cooking, and eating provide this sense of family and closeness.

In terms of finding the right time and place for conversation, again, the key element is awareness of others. Obviously for all of us, our conversational life is a mixture of both private and public encounters. By considering the other person first, you can maintain good relations in both circumstances.

Conversation in a public place depends on the number of others around, your level of comfort, and what kind of conversation you are having. You have to exert a certain amount of energy to protect your conversational space. If you're in a loud restaurant, you may have to raise your voice. If you don't want other people to hear, you may sit closer to your partner, or mask your communication so that others can't understand— for example, by speaking another language.

Yet a public setting can also be invigorating. You may feel energized by the people around you. If you are celebrating, you might pick a particularly boisterous environment to support your achievement. The appropriate public setting can stimulate the flow of conversation. The decor, the music, the food, and the drink enrich your conversational experience.

The more private and sensitive your interaction, the less comfortable you'll feel expressing yourself where you might be overheard. If you feel you may have crossed the line, look to the other person as a barometer. If he or she seems uncomfortable, keep the conversation simple and light and find a new location for a deeper discussion.

You may sometimes choose to have a conversation in the great outdoors. A mountain lake, the beach, or a bench in the park—these environments create a natural sense of space and openness that clears your head and connects you with nature. This simple, elemental connection certainly affects your conversations. In the woods, they may feel more pensive. By the ocean, they may feel more carefree. In a meadow, they may feel more spacious and relaxed. You may choose different words or pause longer between thoughts without feeling odd. Your relationship to the other person may feel different because there is a third party in the conversation: nature itself.

Some conversations are difficult to have because your feelings are so strong you worry about what will happen if you bring up a troubling subject. This fear can make both people freeze. Sometimes it helps to say, "Why don't we go for a walk and talk about it?"

The very act of walking makes us less intensely focused on each other, and strong emotions can be openly expressed in a way that is often hard to do in an enclosed space like an office or at home. The constant movement eases our thoughts and feelings, and the open air and surroundings help keep the conversation fluid. When we are walking together, we find it less awkward in those moments when neither of us has anything to say. Because we're still walking together, these moments don't feel like breaking off contact. Then, when we're ready to return to the main conversation, it's easier to find our way back.

Conversation can occur in a physically intimate setting, such as lying in bed with a loved one or holding hands on a park bench. Within these moments, there is already an atmosphere of connectivity and trust. Such opportunities are essential to the health of close relationships.

Time is an important component of conversation. For example, at a party or dinner, we can relax with our conversational partner because we have time. Because we know that the other person is also there to enjoy the evening, the conversation can meander from topic to topic. However, if we meet someone on the street while shopping, we probably have only a few minutes to talk and should keep the conversation precise and simple. If we try to have a conversation when the other person is carrying groceries or has a child in tow or is clearly in a rush, we are doing so at their discomfort. If we have a lot to discuss, we can make a date to meet later.

Be sensitive to the constraints of time. Even at a social gathering, it may be that our conversational partner has others to talk to. Forcing continued conversation will most likely put the other person into an unreceptive mood. Relating to time appropriately is important. Don't cling. By clinging to your habitual patterns, you are abandoning the art of conversation and windhorse is depleted.

Be mindful of where you are. In certain places, it is important to strike up a conversation—for example, when you are seated next to someone at a dinner party. In other places, conversation may be inappropriate—for example, when the environment is very loud or very quiet, such as at an exciting sporting event or in a packed movie theater. At other times, engaging in conversation may be intrusive because the other person is in pain or emotionally unavailable, or you have introduced a topic better discussed elsewhere. Be aware of these elements. Simply by paying attention, you can often determine whether conversation is appropriate.

Reflection

Reflect on how your conversations vary throughout the day. How do your early morning conversations differ from those in the heat of the day or the coolness of the evening? What are their qualities? By maintaining conversation throughout all these periods, we are developing a good habit and a daily practice.

Posture and Dress

In general, one should be aware of the physical space of others, and our awareness might vary depending on their culture. Becoming overly enthusiastic in conversation and invading the personal space of another can be off-putting, to say the least. In some cultures, such as India, people like being close; standing too far away might offend them. In others, such as the United States, people standing close brings a feeling of claustrophobia. The astute conversationalist will take the cue about physical space from the body language of the person with whom he is speaking.

Hold good posture during conversation. The most direct and engaged posture is when we stand and face each other. When both participants are standing, there is natural respect and energy. Having good eye contact, we see each other's facial expressions and hand gestures. These paint a picture that allows both people to participate.

While sitting, it's best to face the person, or at least sit close enough that you don't need to raise your voice or make gestures to get her attention. By maintaining uplifted posture and good eye contact, you've signaled that you're engaged and curious. If you are slouching, staring out the window or at your phone, or looking around the room, it's clear you've lost interest.

Whether we're standing or sitting, even a few moments of conversation can provide genuine human contact. This is what we're really seeking in all those e-mails and texts. Yet even when we're face-to-face, we can't have heartfelt or personal exchanges when the conversation digresses into verbal bantering interspersed with random thoughts concerning other interests. Digital activity such as looking at Facebook, writing an e-mail, or texting splits our attention, which naturally affects conversational quality. If the conversation is important, reduce or eliminate other activities to focus on it.

In general, the body language should be uplifted. We should learn to make gestures that have dignity and grace, such as leaning forward with interest in a conversation. When we're self-involved, the tension shows in our body. Crossing your arms in front of your chest suggests that you're protecting yourself from the world. It makes us unapproachable and generally reduces our ability to enjoy. When we are self-attached, there is a tendency to be sloppy and casual. In general the body should be an expression of our mental ability to be awake. As a gesture of respect for others, take care with your grooming and dress. It's not that you should dress well to soothe your ego, and it's not about having expensive clothes. Your clothing and appearance is a way to increase your confidence and dignity. It defines who you are and imparts a sense of discipline fitting to both your body and the occasion. Wearing appropriate clothing is like wearing a suit of armor. How you dress can actually invoke upliftedness, grace, and power.

Clothing is not simply about what is comfortable for us; it's about what others see and feel from our presence in their lives. It gives others insight into how we handle ourselves, conveying laziness and carelessness or discipline and exertion. A sloppy approach toward dressing carries the sense that we don't have to follow any rules, that it doesn't matter what we wear or when we wear it. We can come as we are and do whatever we want. Such casualness represents the arrogance of complete individuality that is without regard for others. However, when we choose clothing with care, considering both the occasion and the views of others with respect, we exude gentleness and dignity. This is the notion of beauty.

It is said that in a dark age, people stop appreciating bright colors and wear black and gray, muted tones. Life takes on a mechanized quality—not mechanized in the positive sense of good technology that helps life, but in the sense of being without feeling: monotonous, confused, and muted. A drab environment naturally affects the mind and health. Fortunately, we can counteract the overall tendency toward darkness by cultivating the light of kindness through good conversation.

Reflection

Appreciate the beauty and expression of your clothing. Consider dressing to be your everyday art. Experiment with conveying lightness with colors. Tune in to their sensory qualities and match them to your intention and/or to the occasion. Consider how a proper fit feels. What effect does clothing have on your awareness when you talk to someone else?

Consider Your Partner

The character and arc of your conversation will vary according to your conversational partner.

With friends, the dynamic is simple. There is often much shared experience and camaraderie. It is easy to find something to talk about. You don't feel awkward; you are able to speak freely. On the downside, there could be an overfamiliarity, which leads to the conversation becoming habituated. The friendship creates a cozy safety net, a kind of mutual cocoon. You might end up having variations of the same conversation again and again. If there is love, respect, and kindness, having familiar conversations repeatedly can be healthy and helpful. However, if they incite irritation or numb your curiosity, you could become jaded. This can lead to a feeling of dullness, which means you and your friend have fallen asleep. The antidote is to find some new common ground to explore.

With friends, there may be a competitive streak. One of you starts a new business and the other feels intimidated or jealous. The point is to watch what you do with the feeling. Do you use it to provoke, or do you channel it into curiosity about the business, or even happiness for your friend? With sensitivity and skill, even when you're feeling a strong emotion you can keep having a conversation, and the relationship can remain enjoyable for a long time.

Conversely, when engaging a new acquaintance, you don't know if you have common interests. Because you are unfamiliar with him, the conversation can be awkward. For example, by raving about the hamburger you had for lunch, you discover that your new acquaintance is a vegetarian. On the upside, in meeting new people, you encounter new experiences and stories. These can help you develop broader empathy and insight. However, it does depend on finding common interests. Otherwise, conversation is difficult.

How do you make a genuine connection? There are a few styles to avoid. An invitation to "tell me more about you" (or the subject at hand) is an expression of curiosity, but if you don't reciprocate in your own way, you're just pretending to connect. Eventually your partner will feel as if he's being mined for information. Conversations where you're trying to pry out bits of information without offering any of your own belong in the realm of espionage.

In fact, during times of war, the art of conversation has often been a highly sought-after skill because people with special linguistics training can determine by talking to someone whether he or she is a native or a spy. But it doesn't take a code breaker to figure out whether your conversation partner is genuinely engaging. If she's responding with rejoinders like "I agree" and "I see what you mean," she might appear to be interested, but if she's not adding anything of her own, she's actually keeping her distance. Without equal give-and-take, it's more like a monologue or an interrogation. On the other hand, when there's some sense of real trueness taking place, it feels good.

In conversations between people of different genders, we may perceive the world differently, depending on what is important at their period of life. This inevitably creates different outlooks. Again, use sensitivity, find common ground, and empathize. That ground is necessary for acknowledging differences. If we leap into the differences without it, our conversation might turn out to be pretty short. But if we try to have a conversation while ignoring the differences, the elephant in the room may keep us from genuinely communicating.

The more intimate the relationship, the more deeply we can communicate. Feeling less formal or stiff, we engage with ease. It takes little effort because we already share friendship and affection. But we may take the other person for granted. Since we know each other's habits, our windhorse may be low. Without curiosity and effort, our intimacy cannot grow. The relationship may go stale or even end.

Intimacy is about giving as well as getting. A proper exchange is based on love and also trust. Both parties need to be committed to the principle of relationship. Unlike a negotiation, relationship indicates a continual exchange without a particular result. Of course, things need doing in a relationship, but innately a relationship is ongoing and endless. There's no climax or finality. It's more like walking than sprinting.

If we believe everything's been said, it's more likely that we're not making time to converse, and that there's a lot we still don't know about each other. We're in a habitual pattern because we stopped exploring when we got together, or perhaps we always talk about the same things.

Conversation in marriage does more than help us communicate and solve problems, it also meets one of our most important emotional needs—the need to talk to someone. To bring freshness in, schedule time for conversation. Use it as a way to get to know your spouse further. Show interest in his or her deepest feelings. If you're not used to really talking, this can be a process of building trust. Cultivate interest in each other's favorite topics. Or create new interests: decide what you'd like to learn more about and share books on that topic. Take a class together. Or try engaging your spouse in a conversation about a part of his or her life that doesn't include you—for example, what does he most enjoy about meditation?

Conversation with younger people requires different skills. Here we are setting an example. Through our storytelling, analogies, examples, and reactions, we are communicating our ethics and our view of life. We become a teacher or a guide. Our conversations make more of an impression. So it is important to know the interests of the younger person. Ask what it is that she is most excited about right now. What is it about that thing that she likes best? Who inspires her?

When having conversation with those who are older than us, the dynamics are shifted. Because they have more experience, respect and appreciation are important. It's polite to first give the older person some space to ask you some questions or say something to you. If he doesn't make the first move, ask him about his family, or how he spends his free time. What kind of exercise do you like? What are you reading?

Conversation with teachers, whether in education or trade, usually has the backdrop of both respect and knowledge. At the same time, the conversation does not always have to regard the topic at hand; we can simply appreciate each other's humanity. Respecting our relationship as student and teacher, we would like to learn something about our teacher's approach to life. We can start a conversation by asking her how she makes decisions. Do you put more trust in facts or in feelings? Are you pleased with most of your decisions?

Conversations with spiritual teachers allow us to communicate and exchange with them at a human level, where the transfer of spiritual knowledge continues to occur. It is not necessary to constantly discuss esoteric points. Although you may want answers to burning spiritual questions, the teacher may be more interested in learning more about where you are from, and who your family is. Rather than having an intellectual conversation, he might want to talk about his dog or the weather. As the Shambhala principle tells us, the highest truth is here now, in the most ordinary way. Let us never forget the considerate rituals of simply being with each other.

My wife and her sisters attend formal gatherings where they sometimes sit next to a *khenpo*—a learned scholar in the Tibetan Buddhist tradition—who, despite his or her great learning, can be challenged by having a simple conversation. With so much knowledge of esoteric or academic matters, it can be difficult for a scholar to relate on a human level by talking about ordinary things.

If you already know your conversational partner,

you'll have a history of past encounters, with familiar topics and experiences. That makes it easier to converse, and because there are many shared experiences, some things may not need to be said. Still, there is always an opportunity to bring freshness to any situation. For example, "What was the first movie you ever saw?"

We can also talk about communal experiences that demand our respect. Topics like sex, power, money, birth, and death can activate deep feelings. Each represents something so potent that it carries a certain force field laden with historical and cultural intensity as well as our own emotional experiences. Furthermore, these words can carry personal baggage. Unless we know our partner really well, we may not want to enter such discussions because their intensity reveals part of who we are. Then we either bury these themes deep inside, where they become emotional time bombs that make us very uptight, or out of frustration, we talk about them excessively in an attempt to diminish their power. Inviting another to engage with these realities through conversation helps us deepen our understanding and respect for these themes. Conversation is a way of understanding their energy.

All conversational partners have one thing in common: humanity itself is the binding principle.

Reflection

Reflect on how you would encourage children, people you are mentoring, and students. What are the ways you can bring out their inherent goodness when they are about to engage in a simple task, an unfamiliar task, or a challenging one?

Choose a Topic

Each subject of conversation has its particular quality. When we discuss different subjects, our conversational skill becomes well rounded, which in turn affects our character. Because each of us has special areas of interest, we may tend to have conversations on the same subject again and again. If we tend to socialize with the same group, conversations may dwell on the same subjects. Depending on people's skills, conversations on the same subject could become intricately interesting or repetitively boring. However, because we will inevitably be meeting people of different interests, age groups, understanding, and cultures, a broad conversational palette is beneficial. Here are some examples of different conversational subjects that appeal to everyone.

HEALTH. With someone you already know, an immediate, effective way to have a conversation is to ask how she is feeling. Most people like to talk about themselves, and asking how they're doing shows care. Asking about someone's health helps us bond quickly and demonstrates empathy. One's health is a subject that is readily available. People also love sharing their diet and exercise schemes.

WEATHER. The weather is something that affects everyone. It is an excellent and simple topic of conversation and a good ice breaker—no pun intended. If the weather is good, both individuals can celebrate that fact. If the weather is bad, they can commiserate. The weather is a wonderful jumping-off point for other subjects such as, "Last summer when it was so hot, I remember . . ." It can easily lead to the subject of clothing, fashion, food, or plans. It creates a sense of community, and anyone can easily discuss it.

SPORTS. Sports can be an excellent subject of conversation because they take our attention away from work and are associated with enjoyment. It is an easy way of offering information about yourself or learning about someone else. It is easy to bond over sports, a safe subject that has energy. Generally, a conversation about sports alleviates serious talk. It's simple: a team is either losing or winning. Even rooting for rival teams provides good conversation.

The drawback to talking about sports is that some people are intimidated by physical activity. If they are highly intellectual or not physically oriented, they may have little to say. However, there are a variety of sports to discuss, from active to inactive, and the topic can also include board games and cards, all of which come under the general category of enjoyment.

ART. Art can be an excellent topic of conversation because it can include people's impressions about a variety of forms, such as music, painting, and literature. It holds interest for many people, both educated and uneducated, and with such diverse subject matter, discussions can be very broad. The drawbacks are that some people may feel too intimidated because they are unfamiliar with the language of art or are uncomfortable talking about its subtler aspects. However, in general, discussion of art fosters sophistication and imagination, allowing for a more insightful, less logical aspect of our being to emerge.

WHAT'S HAPPENING IN YOUR NEIGHBORHOOD. If you live in the same place, local events or trends are something to talk about because all you have to do is look around and see what's happening. Are there a lot of new buildings going up? Who will be living in them? What do you think of the new library?

CLASSES AND HOBBIES. Talking about what you are learning and how you spend your free time can be a fascinating door into each other's interests and lives.

FAMILY. Talking about family is a good way to get to know someone and bond with him. It creates a sense of community. Although at times it feels intrusive—there may be familial problems or issues—people often want to talk about their children and how they are doing. The same goes for pets.

FRIENDS. Discussing friends or acquaintances in a conversation is a good way to reveal who your acquaintances are, and to explore what friends you might have in common with your conversational partner.

TRAVEL. Talking about where you've been or where you're going can lead to many other topics, such as the kind of food your conversational partner likes, how often she travels, the type of climate she prefers, and what she does in her spare time.

HISTORY. Discussing history is a good way to keep in touch with the past. It is also a great way of bringing what one has read or studied into a conversation, shedding perspective on what's happening now.

CURRENT AFFAIRS. Current affairs can be an excellent but challenging topic of conversation, an opportunity to explore different perspectives on the events of the day. The drawback is that matters relating to politics can be divisive, and people can become emotional. Also, there is such an endless stream of news these days that some people may prefer not to talk about current affairs. Another drawback is that current affairs can be very complicated at times; therefore, people may not know what is happening at a given time, or they may not be interested. However, it is an excellent way to demonstrate that we are aware of what is happening.

OTHER TOPICS. Talking about the environment—nature, the climate, and natural changes—creates a sense of global community. Talking about books is an excellent way to share our knowledge of subjects we've encountered in our reading. There are always new and fascinating technologies to discuss, as well as science and inventions, whether it be exploring space or the depths of the ocean. Cooking can be an engaging topic of conversation. So can physical and martial arts, which could range from the tea ceremony to archery, boxing, or kung fu. Gardening and landscaping is a popular topic, as working with the soil and plants connects us to the earth. And we can always rely on the topic of entertainment, discussing movies, plays, and music, as well as the celebrities and other well-known people who create them.

True Listening

It is said that when the Buddha first taught, two deer approached, knelt down, and raised their ears. They symbolize the act of listening, a sublime way of being present in the moment. Their perked-up ears represent keen attentiveness. Their bodies kneeling down represent relaxation and respect. The receptive state of listening is a way of learning, a way to gain wisdom and insight. It is auditory meditation in which we focus with our ears. It is being open to genuinely hearing the other with inquisitiveness.

True listening is a skill that we develop. It is not always easy. In this era of technological communication and emotional unavailability, all too often there is more speaking than listening. Frequently, when we are speaking to another, we are not having conversation as such but rather an exchange of rhetoric based on strong opinions. If both participants are speaking, then no one is listening. For a genuine dialogue to occur, both speaking and listening must play leading roles.

The verb *to listen* is connected with the verb *to hear*. Like sight, sound is a direct way for us to know something. By knowing something, we gain wisdom and insight. As well, when we are listening, we are in a receptive state, absorbing and hosting the sound. Seeing, smelling, and hearing are all ways by which we gain information. So engaging in conversation is training in sensitivity—literally, learning to use our senses. Like sonar in a submarine, our senses help us navigate our surroundings, allowing us to accurately place ourselves. When we're not listening, we're not using our ears to gain information and knowledge from the environment. We are feeling our way through the dark, depending on thoughts and concepts in our head.

Unfortunately, our modern culture is in danger of producing a future where there is less listening. At the same time, there is a tendency to indulge in self-expression. It seems that we must all have an opinion. As a result, we rush to express ourselves in our blogs and tweets, but there are so many that no one is listening. We're really too busy listening to ourselves. Yet hearing is one of the most powerful methods for directly understanding what's going on with someone else.

We often have conversations just because we need someone to hear what we have to say. However, in our busy, speedy world it can be difficult to find someone to listen because the act involves placing one's mind on another person. In fact, these days we often hire people to listen to us. Coaches and therapists are trained in the art of listening, providing the space in which to simply express ourselves. To sit quietly and listen demonstrates strength. Their listening enables our stress, fear, worries, and insecurities to be aired. Talking in a context like this can even help us make decisions. However, in conversation, two people are equal partners in both listening and speaking.

By learning to listen in everyday conversations, we can digest, contemplate, and engage in the thoughts of another, understanding and responding to his emotional state. Ultimately this scenario has an innocent root: human beings simply must communicate. For that to happen genuinely, listening and speaking need to be balanced. The ear itself is meant to decipher sounds to communicate feeling, and the inner ear is responsible for balance. Listening helps us balance our relationships.

Think of it in terms of music. If a song had an endless series of notes without a breath or a pause, it wouldn't be music. Some say that the true beauty of music exists in the spaces between the notes. Listening is like those spaces, moments of silence where we listen to what comes before and after.

When speaking, you're more active; when listening, you're more receptive. The exchange is the playful dance of two interlocking human minds, which naturally creates harmony. A conversation in which someone is speaking but no one is listening fosters disharmony—within the conversation and the relationship. Ultimately, listening is the price you pay if you want to be heard.

As in any other activity, it helps to practice listening. The best way is to learn to hold your seat. Tune into the words with your ears and just be there, on the spot. The power has been handed over to the speaker, who is now directing the conversation's mood and energy. You can even imagine yourself as one big ear, with nothing on your mind, as the conversation takes its own direction. Expect the unexpected.

If you feel insecure about your role as the listener, you may not be able to listen with an open mind because you feel intimidated and anxious. You might keep having thoughts about what you want to say and interrupting the conversation in order to regain control. Holding your seat is a process of engagement and self-assurance. It expresses your discipline, particularly in controlling your speech, especially in a conversational setting where the purpose is to enjoy the volley of words and ideas. When it's your turn to listen, it is clearly the other person's opportunity to serve. Ironically, listening often requires a greater sense of confidence than speaking. A good listener is not threatened when another takes the reins of power.

TUNE IN

When we're unable to listen, a number of things are occurring. The first is related to time: we're unable to be in the present. Listening requires us to be on the spot, engaged and attentive. It also requires us to feel and to care. That's where mindfulness comes in. When we don't care and we're inattentive—and thus we can't hear—our minds are focused on ourselves. We care more about our thoughts than what the speaker is saying, allowing memories of past experiences to interfere with our present act of listening.

Abduction by flashback can happen quite harmlessly: you ask a friend about the food at a new restaurant. She says it's good and casually mentions liking the fish tank in the entryway. Fantasizing about the fish you saw while snorkeling on vacation, you cease to care about your friend's story, and by the time you come back to her words, she's describing dessert. The future can also take us far afield when we put our mind into planning what to do next.

At the least, daydreaming while someone else is speaking is a subtle form of rudeness. And in tuning out of the conversation to rehash old memories, we are slowly ingraining the tendency to be jaded. The present moment and other people are not interesting, so we are less available to new stimuli. We forget that conversation is not simply about following dialogue, but also about caring for someone and appreciating our interaction. While it is important to plan for the next day and enjoyable to reminisce about the past, it is inappropriate to become lost in thought when we are having a conversation. Remembering to stay connected is mental decorum.

Another form of not listening is being self-absorbed with a tinge of aggression. In this type of antilistening, we simply disregard what the other person is saying and proceed with our own agenda. We barge ahead with what we're going to say, ignoring the other person's thoughts, feelings, insights, and emotions. Or perhaps we listen to her first few words and rush to our own conclusion. We may think simply, *"Here she goes again."* "Knowing" what someone is about to say and not allowing her to say it is simply rude.

You may think you're saving someone time by pretending to read his mind and move the conversation along. However, as is said, "There's no time like the present." Your partner's words may be different from what you're thinking. Running over them is not good communication. This pattern can be damaging to any relationship, but your life could depend on it should you try it with a doctor, for example. Even with someone you know well, though she may have expressed something similar before, she may now be expressing it in a slightly different way, giving rise to new insight.

Again, listening is simply being there fully with other people. What they have said in the past is the past, and if it sounds the same now, it might be because you never listened. As a result, they have to say it over and over again. The most you can do is listen now and then try to express your understanding so that they will no longer feel the need to say it. Then you can change the subject.

FOCUS
Always put your attention on other people, with your ears focused on their words. Although there may be music, other conversations, birds chirping, and dogs barking, be specific in your focus. A focused mind enhances any experience. Let the other sounds in the room fade as you zoom in on your partner's face, words, and body language.

In order for this focus to occur, relax. We often don't listen well because there is tension in the body. This tension is related to fear and stress. Something is preventing you from truly listening. Perhaps you don't fully trust the other person, so you're not ready to be receptive. Or perhaps you don't respect them, so you're not ready to be submissive. Or maybe you're just worried about something that's occupying your mind, and so you're not available at the moment. To focus and relax, let these things go.

When attempting to listen, take a moment to make the intention to listen. As in any other activity, be neither too tight nor too loose. If your listening becomes too intense, it might spook the other person. If you're too distant, the other person loses interest. Remain distraction free—no phones, televisions, or books. Create an atmosphere of silence, which is the stage on which the speaker enters; it's the signal that he has your attention and respect.

When you listen in a tight mode—all tensed up, holding yourself in, afraid or unwilling to be touched—you may be hearing only a fraction of what the other person says, and the conversation becomes stingy. The flow of energy is meager. For example, she says, "I'm happy to see you," and you're silent, unwilling to reciprocate. You're not allowing yourself to celebrate life. Instead, you are robbing yourself of the celebration that is moment to moment. There is no bigger moment or lesser moment than now.

In the tradition of warriorship, to celebrate moment to moment is called discipline. Discipline is not a sense of oppression or being punished; it is freedom from our own self-perpetuating laziness. In this case I define laziness as the notion of not wanting to be present. You don't quite want to be here, so you're tight. This kind of discipline is necessary in a conversation, and even in sports. In running, you have to be present; otherwise the world gives you feedback—you trip.

When you find your mind wandering during a conversation, check your posture. When you're slumping or shrinking, you're more likely to be distracted. Tuning in to your body sensations and sense perceptions brings you into the present. Or bring yourself back to the conversation with a question: "I'm sorry, I lost focus. Can you say that again?" It is never a mistake to show you are interested.

To listen better, it can be helpful to inhale or exhale, sit down or stand up, uncross your arms or legs, or touch and feel the place of tension in your body. After reconnecting with the body through your posture or breath, you may find yourself relaxed enough to listen and hear.

CARE AND ACCOMMODATE

The noble qualities of a good listener can overcome many of the faults of a poor conversationalist. Try actively sensing what is most important in what the person is saying to you, and ask him more about that. Or step out of your mood by trying to visualize the other person's experience in order to understand him more deeply. Listening may be a receptive act, but it is simultaneously a dynamic endeavor that allows everyone to grow.

Even though listening is a quiet act, you can be warm and show interest, occasionally interjecting, "Is that so?," "I see," or even a few brief sentences reiterating what your partner said: "So after school you traveled to India. Then what did you do?" This is how she knows you're listening. Having listened fully, let your partner know that you heard her. Find a way to share the essence of what she said. "Here's my understanding of what you just said. Did I get it right?" Or make it clear you understood her by sharing thoughts or responses when it seems appropriate. If she seems to want you to respond, you can respond. Then it's her turn to practice listening.

HEARING AS TRANSMISSION

Because I am a spiritual teacher and leader, people assume that I speak a lot. At times, I do give lectures and answer questions. However, I spend a great deal of time listening to people's questions, concerns, opinions, and complaints. This is often a practice in itself—just being there, not necessarily reacting to everything that is said.

Also, in the 2,500-year history of Buddhism, all the

teachings were passed on orally. In the Tibetan tradition, this practice, known as a *lung,* is still very much alive. I have spent hours, weeks, and months sitting and listening to various texts being read. These transmissions occur in a formal setting. The person reading the *lung* is generally a prominent teacher and holder of that tradition. The text could be very brief or thousands of pages long, and reading it aloud can take from a few minutes to a few months. As this happens, one simply listens and hears the words, refraining from getting distracted, falling asleep, or studying other material. This is a great exercise in being present. When the *lung* is finished, then one has full permission to study that text, and has become a recipient of that wisdom and tradition. That means one can study, contemplate, and practice the teachings within that text.

Some listeners are so talented that almost anything they hear immediately goes into memory; they can recite verbatim what someone said. In fact, many of the sutras—the teachings of the Buddha—were written down by attentive disciples who began with the words "Thus have I heard." Mahayana Buddhism would be very different and very short if they had said, "Thus did I not listen." Clearly, some of us will make better speakers and some of us will make better listeners. There must be a reason why we have two ears but only one mouth.

Reflection

When we think we are listening, there may be at least four other things we are doing. Reflect on your habitual listening patterns.

- Are you judging what's being said? (Is it right or wrong?)
- Are you comparing what the person is saying to see if it matches your own experience?
- Are you making a choice? (Do I like what the person is saying or do I dislike it? Come to think of it, do I like this person or not?)
- Are you coming to a decision? (Do I agree with what this person is saying?)

These mental activities tend to gather momentum. Then we are no longer listening. We are making up our minds. In fact, we are often so eager to speak, we can't hold on any longer, so we interrupt.

Praise Is a Gift

It is generous to compliment another. It shows we're not verbally stingy. When we are emotionally frugal, even if people in our life do something magnificent, we are either too self-absorbed or maybe too jealous to compliment them. By handing over power through praise we demonstrate magnanimity, recognizing and confirming another person's good qualities.

Although praise is focused on someone else, it highlights your own good character. First, praise shows you're capable of going beyond self-absorption. You've extended yourself through a gesture of appreciation. Second, it shows that you understand the qualities of good and worthy actions. If you compliment your friend for finishing her exam, it shows respect for knowledge. Complimenting your brother for helping a sick friend shows respect for compassion. Praising your daughter for making her bed demonstrates that we value work and discipline.

Praise comes from confidence in our own worthiness, through which we are empowering others. It increases their energy and self-esteem. By encouraging other people to do good and beneficial acts, we are engaging in society, strengthening its moral and ethical fiber.

In society and in a relationship without compliments or praise, our desire to do better is diminished because our work is taken for granted. If we refrain from giving praise because we think it will go to someone's head, we should realize that conversation may not be the time to teach humility. But withholding praise that has been earned can signal our desire for control or our emotional stinginess. If we can't bother with an opportunity to uplift someone's day with a few simple words, perhaps we're just too insecure.

True praise is genuine. A hollow compliment comes across as tepid and forced, as if we are unavailable or withdrawn. If we aren't really interested in the other person, we are not really engaging. Our energy is low, and we can't rise to the occasion. If we consider our words carefully rather than just saying whatever comes to mind, we'll sound more sincere, which inspires the recipient to respond in a meaningful way. For example, if you praise his cooking, your dinner host might describe how a documentary on Italian food inspired him to use more fresh vegetables.

A compliment is a simple way of acknowledging someone's hard work and is often a doorway to better understanding her. In general, we don't often get the opportunity to compliment others on monumental achievements like winning the Pulitzer Prize or saving a life; fortunately, it is just as important to offer praise for small and mundane daily events. Compliments such as "That was a very clear presentation," "It was brilliant how you moved the office," "Fiona's grades are so much better now that you talked with her teacher," or "I see you have succeeded in losing weight" show social grace because they create warmth, and the other person feels good.

At times we feel as if we fail more than we succeed, so appreciation is a welcome respite from life's vicissitudes. Because people are often unaware of how far their accomplishments have reached, it helps when someone else shines the light on what they've done. In a dark age, people tend to focus on others' faults and shortcomings. The art of conversation involves illuminating others' good qualities. It is only through discovering the wealth of our good qualities that we begin to truly appreciate good people and good things.

If we think compliments are unnecessary because we believe others already know how we feel, we may come across as insensitive or rude. At the same time, when a compliment has a patronizing tone, it may seem like only half a compliment because we're unable to overcome our own pride. Instead of saying, "Good toast!" we say, "So, you finally learned how to make a good toast." Thus what was meant to be a socially gracious gesture is actually an insult. A compliment should not be used as a Trojan horse for expressing our own discontent, for complimenting another can open up a pathway of vulnerability. Hurting someone with a halfhearted compliment shows you're holding some kind of grudge, and it plants the seeds of an adversarial relationship.

Conversely, when praise is heartfelt, it is delightful to celebrate and share the accomplishments of others. Also, compliments allow for criticism to happen without it seeming harsh or unfair. In any case, bringing attention to someone's faults doesn't always lead to change. However, doing so within a context of appreciation offers validation and hope for improvement because appreciation boosts self-esteem.

Even in a brief conversation, a few words of praise can affect the direction of another's life. It is the same in raising children. In this light, the compliment is an essential tool at home because it demonstrates that a child's conduct or achievement is noticed and rewarded. It kindles a feeling of joy at having done something well, which is an incentive for continuing to do it. In the workplace, good leaders know how to use compliments strategically to invigorate the windhorse of colleagues and staff. Likewise, when an ineffective leader is stingy with gratitude, the workforce feels uninspired. Simple comments such as "That was a great report" energize others because they know that you're paying attention, and that if you see what people do well, you will also detect what people do poorly. This is demonstrating good leadership by compliment.

Many of us have a hard time accepting appreciation because somehow we don't feel worthy, so we hit a return volley. If your flash response is to say, "No, I didn't do that great a job, really," or you bounce back with a reciprocal but random compliment, such as "Thanks, I like your haircut!," you are rejecting someone's offering. Be fully present to receive the compliment, with awareness of how it is delivered and expressed, and in what environment, as well as who is offering it. Remember, a compliment is a gift; to accept it with grace has the effect of pleasing the giver. If you become flustered when receiving positive feedback, see a compliment as a signal to stop and compose your mind before opening your mouth.

On the other hand, it will be awkward and strange if you appear to be fishing for compliments. If someone likes your scrambled eggs and says, "You're a good cook," and you respond by saying, "Tell me more. Are they better than your mom's?," a simple compliment has turned into an ego-boosting session. A heartfelt "Thank you" or a humble "Oh, that's very kind of you" or "I'm glad you enjoyed it" is always appropriate.

Be sensible about praise. Compliments can quickly devolve into insincere attempts at ingratiating yourself, and you might cross the line into attempting to acquire something by flattery. Praise is honest and genuine, with a quality of generosity and release. By contrast, flattery is somewhat dishonest, like telling your sister she looks good in spite of her cold in order to borrow her car. It's a form of manipulation to exaggerate another's action for your own benefit—that is, praising people for qualities they don't have or actions they didn't do. Depending on the context, you may come across as offensive, or even as inappropriately flirtatious.

One meaning of *flatter* is "to stroke with the hand, to caress," as if we're trying to tame and soften someone so that they become more pliable for our purposes. It has an element of stickiness and seduction because it's insincere, specifically crafted toward achieving our own ends. The recipient's reaction could range from amusement to offense.

Compliments and praise are spontaneous expressions of appreciation from children, family, or friends. From peers, they are acts of confirmation. From parents or teachers, they are expressions of pride. From our bosses, they are moments of encouragement. From strangers, they are expressions of good social principles.

By encouraging someone's achievements or good qualities, we can rise to any occasion. Praise uplifts the other person's spirits, with the added bonus of uplifting our own.

Reflection

Consider offering sincere praise to someone you wouldn't normally give it to. What would you say? Reflect on how appreciation expressed by others has affected your life—or not.

The Strength of Feedback

How we express our observations is a delicate matter. Critiquing people's ideas can be perceived as an attack on their sense of identity. What you consider to be a simple observation might affect people immediately and dramatically, rendering them incapable of hearing anything else you say. They think you don't like them, or they're struck by some other insecurity.

Giving feedback comes down to skillfully delivering the message. Be clear about what you are critiquing. Don't make general accusations that make people feel as if their character is under attack. Be as simple and accurate as possible in describing what people do. At the same time, be supportive and understanding. Show that you can connect with their feelings, and that you sympathize with their situations. This creates empathy, which helps guide them toward a solution.

When offering feedback, we are engaging in a sensitive and potent exchange. Avoid tones of humiliation. Try not to come across as manipulative or revenge driven. Lead the criticism by mentioning the positive. For example, if you don't like the pasta your spouse cooked for dinner, don't blurt out, "This is gross!" You might say, "What kind of spices did you use tonight?," which opens a dialogue. Your spouse might be more responsive to criticism at that point because you are showing that you have thought about the process he went through.

Often the feeling of inadequacy surrounds how well you perform a particular task. Cooking, parenting, driving, doing the dishes, cleaning, sending e-mails, writing reports, teaching a class, or picking up the dry cleaning—each of these common daily ceremonies comes with a level of self-worth attached.

In fact, a healthy sense of self allows room for improvement. When you learn how to accept a critique—as well as small failures, losses, or disappointments—your daily imperfections no longer make a dent in your self-esteem because you grow from them. Even if you believe that your view of how you're doing things is the only correct one, the observations of others in common daily dealings are also important. Often there is something to be learned from both sides. By the same token, it's better not to be completely fixated or attached to your own ideas or schedule. Otherwise, when situations don't go your way, you could become dislodged. "What can I learn from this?" is always a good question.

When you receive feedback, try to relax, listen to it, and hold your seat. Avoid collapsing, immediately formulating your defense, or attacking others, because often the critique has arisen from their care and concern. Also, when you receive criticism about your actions, don't mistake this for criticism about who you are as a person. Imagine that whoever is giving you feedback is talking about somebody else. If what they are saying sounds true, then simply agree and acknowledge it. Don't waste time and energy creating convoluted ways of deflecting responsibility. At the same time, don't be a martyr by becoming overly self-deprecating. Hold your dignity. After a critique you might say, "Thank you for that. I see what you mean, and I'll definitely think about it."

If you feel the critique was inaccurate or unjust, you might say, "Let me think about that. I'm not sure if it's completely true." Or "I can see why you brought that up, but I'm not sure I completely agree." However, when replying, try not to provoke the situation by counter-criticizing: "It may be that I'm not listening, but you're not paying attention to details, and on top of that, you're insulting me!" Recognize the sensitivity and power of feedback, and try to remain calm and realize that it may be no easier for the other person to give you feedback than it is for you to take it.

One mind-training slogan says, "Of the two witnesses, hold the principal one." You're the only one who knows what's happening in your mind and intention. In fact, it is ourselves who should be most concerned about how we act, because we are most affected by our actions. When I was going into one of my first meditation retreats, I asked my father for some advice. He said, "How you act when you're alone affects everything about the rest of your life."

Often when people are unable to take criticism, they act like children—undisciplined. They react without thinking first. Conversation itself as an act of communicating is a mature endeavor. Even though there is always a child in each of us, and we don't like being told that we're wrong, receiving constructive feedback makes us strong. Taking criticism and utilizing it to develop our character is a great life skill. Absorb it, learn from it what you can, and move on.

Sometimes we are completely closed off to feedback. We are too insecure to hear it, so we don't. Instead, we turn back to a dependable habit that appears to be the most immediate and effective way of reestablishing familiar self-identity: *I am right. Everyone else is wrong.* But that is a way to close down. If instead we can think,

I believe I was right, but clearly, by what others have said, I need to reevaluate, this moment of self-reflection will help us continue to open up and grow.

Reflection

Recall how you've experienced feedback in the past, both positive and negative. Imagine what it is like to be praised and thanked, perhaps even more than is necessary, for something you've done. How do you react? Then reflect on what it is like to receive negative feedback and how you react. Experiment with what it is like to be puffed up or deflated. Now imagine what it is like to remain in the middle, open and relaxed, whatever feedback is received.

Conversation Is Not Therapy, Bargaining, or Debate

CONVERSATION IS NOT THERAPY

In our modern culture, we seem to think a conversation is superficial unless a problem or a painful point is discussed. Conversations become intertwined with divulging aspects of our personal lives. They turn into periods of advice or therapy. Although discussing personal issues is sometimes unavoidable, one person confiding her troubles in another is different from having a conversation. The opportunity for dialogue diminishes in a conversation that becomes a session of problem solving or coming to the rescue.

Every interaction does not have to center on personal problems. In fact, you should be mindful of and careful about in whom you confide. Avoid prying into other people's lives by asking painful questions like "Why did you and Ron split up?" Unless you are a close friend or have been asked to advise, intruding into another's life is not an act of kindness but a lack of self-restraint. Also, when you talk about your problems, people often feel pressured to come up with a solution. Instead of airing your problems or inviting someone else's, keep other topics in mind: books, the latest television series, a new class, your recent vacation, or what's happening in the garden. There are many ways to share our lives beyond focusing on problems.

You may sometimes feel that unless you share a problem, you are not being open or direct. However, genuine connection can take place without divulging all your secrets. Simply exchanging in an atmosphere of warmth can be soothing and beneficial. At the same time, if a friend feels she needs to express her troubles, a good conversationalist can take this in stride.

Reflection

Notice and write down habitual conversations—those that you tend to have again and again. For example, you may tend to talk about work, family difficulties, or the problems of the world. What is your story? Does it change from conversation to conversation? Is there something you'd rather be talking about? Recognizing our patterns allows us to break out of that cycle and create a new story line.

WHEN CONVERSATION *IS* THERAPY

In good therapy, clients learn a new vocabulary that allows them to express themselves on a more profound and deeper level. This is a liberating experience that affects all their personal interactions. They become aware and attuned to their basic goodness and are able for the first time, in some cases, to express themselves appropriately. This is a powerful skill and has ramifications for creating an enlightened society. Good conversation in psychotherapy is a life-enriching and, in some cases, a lifesaving path.

CONVERSATION ISN'T BARGAINING

If our conversation transforms from a warm and communal exchange into a request of the other person, we need to acknowledge that now we are bargaining. If the other person's response tells us we've crossed a line, we should respect the boundaries. For example, if we ask a coworker to help us out of a tight spot and he says, "Sorry, I'm on a deadline today," by persisting, we create an awkward dynamic. Respecting that someone has said no helps maintain good relations.

By all means, avoid asking friends for free professional advice or services.

Reflection

When you must negotiate, are you able to take no for an answer? Are you able to let go of the outcome even if it doesn't meet your expectations?

KNOW WHEN TO SAY NO

In the same light, we should be careful when we too readily agree to do favors for others. Even though conversations are simple by nature, they can become very complicated if they are mismanaged. If we make promises we're unable to fulfill, although initially we come across as helpful, eventually we appear to be unreliable. If you feel pressured by a request, learn to say no. If saying no is hard, practice it. If you remember that good conversation is grounded in sensitivity and respect toward others—including yourself—you are less likely to make mistakes. You're being very impolite to yourself if you automatically say yes to a request because you're not considering your own priorities. Learn to say, "I need to contemplate that. May I get back to you?" If someone asks you to walk the dog while she is on vacation and you know you don't have time, inevitably you will not be able to fulfill your commitment. But if you know the answer is no, it's much more polite to say no than to pretend you're saying yes and then back out later.

Reflection

What are your priorities? Look at what you really need to do in your day—and your life. What's driving your intention in terms of how you use your time? Is it habit, or is it initiative? Do you feel satisfied, or do you want to make changes?

CONVERSATION VERSUS DEBATE

It's important to keep in mind that good conversation is not a debate, but it isn't based on agreeing, either. Rather, it is a way to enjoy being with another person even if we have different values, opinions, and beliefs. In our era, though, debate and conversation have become blurred, which directly affects our ability to listen. Because debate has a more competitive edge, we may feel the need to win every conversation. We demonstrate this by talking more, putting the listener into the position of being the loser. Likewise, if we are not being argumentative and dominating the space, we feel that we are losing face. Clearly, debate can be constructive, and it requires astute listening on both sides, if for no other reason than to unravel the other's logic. But in a debate, we oppose. We are presenting our stance and trying to convince someone of it.

Sometimes talking with another person can seem like a battle: Whose logic is quicker? Who is wittier?

In many cases it is all about suppressing an opponent rather than making friends. To make friends suggests inviting and welcoming people, not competing with, manipulating, or bashing them.

Often what derails a conversation is when a moment of aggression arises and we are unable to handle it. That aggression can arise as anger or lack of patience. Or it can be camouflaged as pride or stinginess. When aggression assumes the mantle, our tongues become the weapon and our words become the soldiers. Naturally, when we start attacking our opponents, unless they are skilled at deflecting aggression, our words plant land mines of aggression in them and an argument inevitably ensues.

In good conversation, there is no winner. If we believe that the point is to win, both partners lose, because a good conversation is rooted in openness. When we enter a conversation with a fixed opinion, determined to convince the other, we are no longer open. When we fail to listen, we are no longer accommodating. In fact, good listening demonstrates good human character. It is the foundation of dialogue, which explores issues on an equal footing and open ground, with flexibility of mind. Wise leaders are often such excellent listeners that their attention and self-assurance can unnerve the speaker.

Reflection

Reflect on your conversation style. Are you debating? Are you trying to win every conversation? On the other hand, do you not speak up because you're afraid of confrontation?

Yes, and . . .

In general, conversation is a time to be gracious and agreeable. This becomes challenging for people who disagree on a topic. It may be that they don't really mean what they say, but by disagreeing they separate themselves from others and create a sense of identity. For example, after many days of rain, when someone in the conversation says, "Isn't it great? The sun has finally come out!," the disagreeable person replies, "I prefer the rain." Although everyone else is enjoying the sun, this person has to disagree in order to seem different. In a slightly contorted fashion, such a person wants to be acknowledged. This makes any conversation difficult.

However, a skilled conversationalist can utilize even awkward answers. For example, we might reply, "Yes, I noticed your raincoat as you came in. Did you get that recently? It looks good on you." When the disagreeable person responds, "Yes. I just bought it, but I hate shopping," we can agree: "Yes, shopping is often very tiring because of the long queues." Saying yes can be a powerful tool in dealing with difficult people. We're not necessarily agreeing with them, but by acknowledging and respecting what they say, we are not separating from them. It helps us make do with whatever the conversation presents. And the formulation "Yes, and" will carry a conversation further than "Yes, but," which throws up a roadblock.

Aggression is trying to solve all scenarios with a sense of us versus them. It is separating self from other. This unnatural division creates dualism, with the tendency to hold and project. For example, if you tend to be a controlling person, you may project that others are trying to boss you around. If you hate and fear someone, you will project that others hate and fear you. It is only the free flow of mingling self and other, "just you and me," that allows for true exchange. A good conversation is the constant embodiment of living in the challenge of never giving up on others. Simultaneously, it is the heroic gesture of not giving up on ourselves.

When feeling irritated in a conversation, instead of reacting, you can ask your partner, "How do others see that?" or "How do others feel about that?" to give yourself time to lessen your reactivity. It is rude to try to force your opinion on someone. Say yes as often as possible, and when you must say no, use it firmly.

Not sure what to say? Silence can be the most potent

language. Sometimes it means you have nothing to say, or you don't know what to say. At other times it means that you know what to say, but you aren't saying it. In some cases, it is better to say less and let the silence speak. In order not to create discomfort, hold that silence with appreciation for the other person and project warmth and confidence. Otherwise, silence can be intimidating.

Conversely, being overly agreeable makes you seem overeager. You may come across as unstable. Luckily, conversations are full of things we like and do not like, and it's fine to gently express a sincere opinion. If you share an opinion, begin with "I feel . . ." or "I think . . ." Stay open. Own what you say. Your genuineness can inspire others to be honest as well. At the same time, a conversation is not the final word. It's important to keep a larger frame of mind and appreciate the benefits of interaction altogether.

For example, one of us may be a staunch vegetarian while another raises animals for food, or perhaps we are affiliated with different political parties. At those points, conversations can be challenging. However, staying with a sense of respect for the other while not abandoning our own principles can bring such conversations to unexpected insights. An almost infectious openness arises around people who have the ability to be themselves and still respect those who are not like them. Cultivate equanimity and warmth. It is remarkably valuable in all sorts of social interactions.

If your conversation partner is making statements that seem obviously false or apparently ridiculous, you can, of course, ask directly about them, which can appear as a challenge. A more interesting mental exercise is to assume for the moment that the person is making a sensible statement about the world, and then ask yourself, *What would have to be true about the world for someone to say something like this?* Try to imagine it from the other's point of view. It will probably not lead to agreement, but it may lead to a feeling of compassion.

There's never going to be one thing we all agree on, but we don't have to hate each other, and we don't have to call each other names. We can disagree constructively, which starts with listening to each other. Keep in mind that there are many ways to see the same thing. When you find yourself in a moment of intense disagreement, rather than narrowing your mind, try to expand it. Even when there is a topic of debate, there can be an art to how we disagree. Often simply acknowledging that the other person has a different point of view is helpful. The one thing you can always share with another? Respect.

If you think you're always right, you might develop a verbal habit of needing to win every argument. This shows your own insecurity and fixity. If you can connect to your heart and breathe, you may become more flexible, and then you won't be as destabilized by disagreements because you won't perceive them as an attack on your character. In life, argument is natural because it is based on people's perspectives, which are constantly changing. We can argue about whether a restaurant was good or bad, or if a movie was good or bad. These arguments are subjective, and do not require us to become offended.

It is helpful to realize that you may not come to a consensus. Once you decide to engage in dialogue with a conflicting viewpoint, you have to be willing to both win and lose. Just as when you enter a competition, you must recognize that the outcome could go either way. If you win, don't gloat, and if you lose, be magnanimous. If you're attached to winning arguments or you're too self-effacing when you lose, lean into that feeling by wholeheartedly engaging in good conversation and continuing to experiment with learning to let go.

Reflection

Think of a conversation where you insisted on your point of view and, in the middle of a heated disagreement, discovered that you'd misinterpreted what someone said and were completely wrong. At that moment, where did all those extreme emotions go?

Avoid Jargon, Insults, Slang, and Gossip

JARGON

The word *jargon* originated with an old French word that meant "chattering"—noisy talk or gibberish. It is connected with the words *gossip* and *twitter*. Like birds chirping, jargon has its own meaning that is not understood by all. We all have our own jargon, as does each geographical region, profession, and age group.

In conversation, try to avoid using jargon, especially if you don't know each other well. Using insider language immediately distances you from other people. It might make them feel insecure because they feel excluded. If you're talking business with a colleague, jargon will inevitably arise, but at that moment the conversation has turned from a social space to a work-related meeting. Even at company socials where one could use endless jargon, it is beneficial for coworkers to enjoy good conversation instead of talking about work. It creates a different pathway of communication and helps people bond in a more universal way. In turn, this deeper connection helps energize our business endeavors.

We see this in diplomacy: when negotiations and jargon fall away, communication happens at a more human level. Ultimately, we are trying to see if the other individual is honest and therefore genuine. In this way, conversation is a truth serum that reveals a tremendous amount of information. If we lie or exaggerate or obscure the truth through jargon, it shows up in our posture and our confidence. Therefore, even in a professional setting, being honest and authentic builds trust that allows for a genuine connection.

INSULTS

Often when we cannot control ourselves, we devolve to rudeness and may insult others. In Latin, the word *insult* means "to jump at"; it is essentially a verbal lunge. Like biting dogs, we cannot hold ourselves back.

Insults exist in all languages. These verbal weapons are intended to inflict damage or cause harm to another's sense of identity or reputation. While an insult may or may not harm another, it definitely damages one's own reputation. Especially if it is profane, this sign of frustration and desperation reflects badly on the person who says it. Our patience has run out, our intelligence has run thin, our imagination has gone dry, so we blurt out words like a blunt instrument.

Some insults can be more sophisticated and shrewd. For example, "I never knew how much I loved you until you let me down." Like layering poison into delicious food, what appears to be a compliment or a sign of affection is simply a decoy by which to carry the insult. When this occurs, the parameters of a good conversation have fallen away. Two adversaries are feeling each other out, preparing for battle. Communication is not being used to build bridges but to tear them down. Although they may appear more educated and studied, even sophisticated forms of insults are still a form of lunging.

At times we all become irritated by what others do or say, but especially in a public setting, insults may not only hurt others but also embarrass them. With that, we immediately plant the seeds of anger and even revenge. The more we insult others, the more costly it will be to repair the damages. We may feel good and self-vindicated in the moment, but later we'll feel remorse and regret. Thus conversation is the constant balance of temperance and consideration.

PROFANITY AND SLANG

Profanity is most commonly used as insults—or in some circles, ironically, as terms of endearment. In general, it is slang—informal language considered inappropriate for more formal gatherings. Slang has its own universe of meaning. We might consider slang to be a more direct or honest form of speech. However, in an inappropriate setting slang can come across as rude. Generally, such language can be aggressive, which means we've most likely given up on gaining any benefit from the interaction. Because a great deal of happiness is based on our relationships, it's best to use jargon only occasionally, slang sparingly, and insults never. Of course we would apply this generality depending on which situation, culture, and relationship we find ourselves in. What are jargon, slang, or insults will certainly change depending on where, when, and with whom we find ourselves.

GOSSIP

Even idle chitchat reveals our character when bits of jealousy, desire, and hostility can be detected. By engaging in such verbal frivolity, we have no idea what chain of events we are starting. Some of it might reach the ears of others, and then we spend months mending friendships. If in fact it is meaningless, then it does not need to be uttered. If it is meaningful, it may be inappropriate to divulge it. Creating vindictive rumors and gossip is not the art of conversation. One mind-training slogan says it simply: "Don't ponder others."

Gossip is a way of maneuvering, positioning ourselves to be in the most favorable spot. It is feeling proud to be above the weak, and pleased when the great fall. If there is ego and confused emotion, there will be gossip. Unbridled gossip is harming others by exposing their faults and laying the ground for revenge. It reveals our inability to control our negative emotions.

However, knowing that gossip is inappropriate, we can express our concerns and pains among family or close friends. Then it is not happening at the cost of another's reputation, and we might gain valuable advice. Warriorship is a path of concern for others and a way of contacting a more expansive mind. Be concerned with the plight of others instead of using information as a tool for gloating. Respect speech. It rides along the winds of space and time, and those winds circle the globe.

Reflection

If you're unable to restrain yourself, and you feel that you need to blurt out something, try to stop and reflect. Is it necessary? Is it kind? Am I simply unable to control myself? In conversation we must practice temperance, the ability to think before we speak.

Avoid Complaint

Once, when I was visiting Orissa, India, I was conducting a ceremony with His Eminence Namkha Rinpoche. He was a close friend of my father's and is a senior lama, or teacher, in the Nyingma lineage. The ceremonies began very early, ended very late, and were physically demanding. One morning, the senior monks were concerned about Namkha Rinpoche's health and asked him to take a break. When I asked him how he was doing, he smiled and said, "No complaints! I'm totally fine."

Many of us are actually fairly healthy, but because we do not trust it, we are always complaining. The problem with complaining is that it always leads to another complaint. Even if we are fine, we start complaining about somebody else: "What's wrong with *them*?" It's endless; it fosters a continual sense of dissatisfaction. In Buddhism this is called samsara.

Samsara always has to have the last word: we need one more thing to make us happy. One thing leads to the next, perpetuated by our desire to have final satisfaction in the next experience. But the next experience feels uneasy, and we still need one more thing. We need to eat, then we need to listen to music, then we need to watch a movie, then we need to relax in a bath. The desire to feel satisfied is a continual process that drives our lives. Samsara is not a sin; it's just what ends up happening. What's happening is called suffering. We keep ourselves on this wheel by generating negative emotions. So we have to watch our minds and our mouths. Otherwise, we will always be complaining.

We all like to commiserate with friends and colleagues occasionally, because in sharing our woes we sometimes experience comfort and release. In commiseration, we empathetically bond over life's difficulties. For example, when a rainstorm causes a blackout, we might say, "Yes, I know. It's amazing how much we depend on electricity. I can't believe how difficult life is without it."

However, chronic complaining is an unhealthy verbal habit that can drain us of our dignity and self-respect. It may also establish a pattern of accentuating the negative. It lacks social grace—by harping on negativity, we begin to spread our disquieted thoughts and display our unhappiness with how we are handling our lives.

To focus on what is wrong with our lives and the world is inconsiderate of others. By subjecting others to our woes, we are forcing them to experience discomfort. During any conversation, no doubt, people are having difficulties, but they do not bring them up because the time does not seem appropriate.

Complaining indicates a lack of peripheral awareness. It can make others feel excluded and it dampens the mood. Obviously, if sad and disturbing things have occurred, they will naturally arise in conversation. But if we use a conversation as a vehicle for complaint, it will be short-lived. Going negative is demanding and claustrophobic. It takes a lot of energy and it keeps us from participating in the positive. Therefore, we should reflect for a moment before engaging in a negative train of thought followed by an avalanche of complaint, which will quickly derail any conversation.

A very common form of complaining is assigning blame. We aren't able to handle difficulty, so we try to alleviate that feeling by shifting the responsibility to others. We might say, "I'm sick of not having electricity. I can't believe how disorganized and slow the power company is." Or "Because they are not doing their job, we have to sit in the dark." This kind of complaining is futile and further promotes a negative environment. It often stems from personal discontentment. Perhaps our relationship is not going well, or we didn't get the promotion, or we're having health or money issues. We try to alleviate our desire for life to be different by shifting the responsibility to others. When we complain, our discontentment is a blanket that we spread everywhere. In reality, not much comes from complaining. The troubles of the world don't go away. Change occurs through having optimism and solving problems together.

Before you start complaining, ask yourself, *Do I truly want to complain? Will it help my friend to hear this?* At that moment, you are in a pivotal situation. On the one hand, life is full of elements that are out of our control. In fact, much of what causes our grief and insecurity, such as the economy and the weather, is uncontrollable. However, we do have some control over how we respond to a situation. When we choose to spread negativity through our own complaint, others feel ill at ease and our relationship is jeopardized. Instead of perpetuating the bad weather in your world, why not just keep quiet?

One method for reducing the habit of complaining is to make a list of everything that is seemingly wrong in your life. From that list, choose one of your routine complaints. Then refrain from indulging in it for a set period of time. This becomes an exercise in letting go. The bravery of letting go leaves some room for a creative solution to arise.

Good conversation is a path of optimism. Others always saying how bad things are could drive our windhorse down. A good reply is, "Yes, I know things are bad, but I can also see that fundamentally it is not that way." This means we are seeing things in a much bigger perspective. In a dark age, we tend to believe in the power of negativity. But as warriors, we know that even negativity has the power to wake us up. Rather than collapsing under the weight of difficulties, we persevere in overcoming them by moving forward. We could try patience instead of anger, exertion instead of envy, generosity instead of grasping.

Peace of mind can only come from yourself. Again, this comes back to bravery. It happens moment to moment in how we handle our minds, our emotions, and our relationships. Can we engage with the spirit of being totally exposed? Can we live every moment genuinely, without a safety net? Whether we can or not, this is how things are. We have to be on the spot, we have to live our life, we have to make decisions. Bravery is being able to hold open the space of possibility. It is raising the gaze and acting like a warrior, even within the vicissitudes of chaos and uncertainty.

Reflection

Try not to complain for an entire day. This may take more discipline than you expect, and it may be that what you think are not complaints are actually hidden complaints. The main thing is to have a sense of humor as you explore letting go of your preconceptions. How does it feel to lighten the burden of complaint?

Happy, Sad, Tired, or Ill

When you are happy, you may have to temper your exuberance for those around you who are not happy or who are having difficulty. Instead of gloating, utilize your happiness to uplift others by engaging them in good conversation.

If you are sad, finding the energy and emotional space for conversation can be difficult. However, putting a little energy into a simple conversation with a friend can help reduce your isolation and lighten your sadness.

If you don't sleep enough, if you're overloaded with problems and decisions, or if your energy is scattered, then you feel you can't ride the situation, and you begin to withdraw and isolate yourself. Everything feels like a challenge and a threat. You avoid conversations and contact with others. Because human interaction is fundamental to life, you feel less connected, less interested, and less alive.

Yet even when you're tired, you can have a good dialogue, especially with family and friends. You don't have to hide the fact that you're tired; there are ways to tell them without necessarily complaining, such as, "That was a very long day, but I'm glad to be home. You look nice. What smells so good?" Even though you had a long day, you're willing to engage. Your conversations might be simpler, even reserved, but putting some energy into good relations strengthens the bond. Likewise, if your partner is tired, you can moderate your speech so that it is soothing, not taxing.

If you feel unwell, rushed, hassled, or insecure, attempts at conversation often don't seem genuine. They may come across as being feeble, hollow, or maybe even aggressive. When someone asks how you are, you snap, "I'm fine!" but it sounds like "Go away!" Truly, there are times when we feel as if we just can't engage with another person. We don't have the energy; we can't deal with that person, or we don't want to waste our breath. But like any other skill, it is good to practice conversation when you're not in peak condition.

How you initiate conversation is a barometer of your energy and life. Be consistent in reaching out and listening to others even during unfavorable times. Keep the pathways of connectivity open. Having a conversation when you're not feeling well can speed healing or soothe pain. Depending on the severity of the illness and your energy level, a simple conversation can boost your mood and relieve your mind from fear, at least briefly, and can help your recovery. Similarly, connecting with a sick friend or acquaintance can help that person. Even though you may feel quite helpless, just being there and listening is a simple way to give support.

Difficult situations bring us closer to life's realities. In my work I often talk with the ill or dying. Even though they are in a weakened state, they often speak with a lot of feeling and emotion because they are appreciating the fragility and preciousness of life. These conversations are very meaningful. They show that instead of cowering from the reality of impermanence, we can rouse confidence in the primordial health and well-being available to us at any point on our journey.

Reflection

Imagine that you are on your deathbed, with only a little breath left in your body. What do you need to say? To whom?

End Well

Good conclusions are important, and this is no different in conversation. Ending a conversation well is usually pretty simple: "It was good to talk to you," "Be well," "I look forward to next time," or "Good luck with that." In Tibetan, when somebody leaves, we say, *"Ka-lee pay,"* which means, "Go slowly." We're saying we're sad to see them go.

Generally speaking, people are happy to meet and sad to depart. At the end of a conversation, we like to acknowledge that the interaction was worthwhile. Depending on the circumstances, a quick nod, a bow, a smile, a handshake, or a hug are simple and gracious ways of conveying our appreciation of the other person. If we will see them again, this feeling creates a sense of looking forward; if we are not so sure we will see them again, it creates an appropriately sad tone.

Even if the other person is in midsentence and we must rush away, we can say, "I'm sorry to interrupt you, but I'm late for my train. It was really good to see you, and I look forward to continuing this conversation." The person may be disappointed, but they will still feel heard and respected.

Ending a conversation well plants the seed for a clean new beginning the next time we see someone. It has an important effect on the dialogue itself. It gives conversation a balance: good at the beginning, good in the middle, and good at the end. With such symmetry, beauty, and harmony, the ideas we shared don't end with the conversation; they continue to percolate. In the same way, ending a conversation poorly has a retroactive effect. Even if many good feelings and ideas were exchanged, the conversation ending poorly somehow stains them. We may forget the good aspects and remember only the poor ending.

If we end conversations poorly by hurling insults or just walking away without a response, we are ending not only the conversation, but also possibly the relationship. If we habitually end conversations poorly, our reputation is affected. Also, the karmic cycle comes around and people tend to walk away when we speak to them.

Particularly when the conversations are important or meaningful, a good conclusion seals the exchange. Each person wants to ensure that the other felt very good about the meeting. At this time, a long eloquent compliment may be appropriate: "After hearing so much about you, having had this opportunity to meet is truly an honor. I wish you much success in your endeavors and look forward to our next meeting." The other person might say: "I, too, appreciated our meeting tremendously; it was very meaningful for me. I certainly hope we can continue the extraordinary dialogue we began today." This exchange can be followed by a bow, hug, or kiss, depending on the culture. Likewise, the exchanging of gifts, business cards, and phone numbers indicates the weight of a relationship and the desire to continue.

At other times, especially between friends and family, separations can make us emotional and difficult. Although not many words may be uttered, there may be crying and other emotional expressions. Generally, impermanence is hard for people to handle. This can always be seen in how we handle the conclusion of things, and conversation is no different.

Reflection

There are lots of ways to end a conversation. Which ones work best for you?

- Make a positive comment: "It's been great talking to you."
- Offer a summary: "I'm really glad we had this opportunity to catch up."
- Share a legitimate excuse: "I've got to get back to work now. I'm due at a meeting."
- At a party, introduce another person into the conversation: "I'm going to mingle now, but before I go, may I introduce you to Cynthia? She's from the Midwest, too."
- Make a plan for the future: "It's been great seeing you. Shall we get together for tea again next month?"

Enrich Your World

Include Others

Many conversations are one-on-one experiences, but that doesn't mean you can't have a good conversation with more than one person. If you are having a conversation at a party and someone walks up and wants to join, it is generous to invite him or her in. For example, if you are discussing last night's game, you could wait for a pause in the conversation, turn to the newcomer, and say, "Kevin, who were you rooting for?" Or greet the newcomer and make introductions. Being gracious helps the other person feel included, acknowledged, and cared for. At a large gathering where many conversations are happening simultaneously, including another person in the mix may simply just be a matter of making eye contact and saying hello. It is the moment of inclusion that is important.

Some places are challenging for conversation. If you're in a loud restaurant, if the weather is extremely hot or cold, or if you're standing in the street, a simple nod, wave, or handshake might be the extent of your communication. At church or the theater, you may simply have to smile, and let that be the conversation. It is still very different in quality from the ambient conversations we are having on social media.

When small children are running around, it may be difficult to talk. However, in these familial settings, the general atmosphere of love allows for conversation and communication to happen in a variety of ways, and if conversations have a fragmented or stop-start quality, by and large nobody takes it too personally. Because we are there for the children, we can either accept the natural end of the conversation, come back to the topic after we've been interrupted, or—if the conversation seems important—make a date to follow it through in a more appropriate place.

Seeing adults in conversation sets a beneficial example for younger family members and provides an opportunity to learn some simple communication skills, even at a young age. And there is no better way to build relationships with children than to talk to them. By having conversations with our children daily, we are teaching them communication skills that are essential for their future happiness. We demonstrate making eye contact, speaking clearly, and listening, and they can learn how to take turns and not interrupt

and how to respond appropriately, as well as how to behave politely when entering or leaving a conversation. Even very young children can learn to say "Hello" and "Good-bye."

One thing children teach us as soon as they're born is that the wish to communicate and connect is natural and innate. Because children are constantly wanting to communicate with their environment and discover the world, this is something we should support. If this inquisitiveness is not encouraged, children tend to withdraw as they age, becoming less curious. As they run around singing, dancing, and banging on walls and tables, children are in fact having quite a good conversation.

Love and compassion, respect and dignity are vital in building a child's character, and parents are in the very powerful role of being able to support those elements. Especially these days, when many people feel a lack of purpose, it is challenging to understand who you are and how you should relate to others. When parents show their willingness to express compassion and kindness, children can feel their own. That's one way these seeds are cultivated. But if feeling is not nurtured, we forget about compassion and kindness, and then spend the rest of our lives trying to rediscover it. Even though human culture has become technologically advanced, we need to explore these fundamental questions. How can we be compassionate? How can we be kind?

Reflection

Think about what words you would use to describe how it feels when you're open and feeling compassion. How about when you're closed? Try describing these in a poetic way in only a few words, and in a prosaic way as a detailed description. Investigate how things feel in the body and how things feel in the mind.

Smile at Life

Good conversation is a way of celebrating the random occurrences in our day. Why is it that we sometimes feel hesitant to celebrate? On such occasions, my father used to say, "Smile," as if that were the path of enlightenment right there.

Why don't we smile more often? We're afraid something bad is going to happen. We might feel exposed, or someone might think we're flirting when we're just being friendly. We're afraid we'll look silly, or simply that our teeth look bad. We're afraid that if we smile, somebody will reject us. We're all suffering in many ways, advertently or inadvertently. The notion of fearlessness is not getting rid of the fear, not getting rid of the unknowing, but being willing to look at it and smile. As Winston Churchill said to his troops, "War is a game that is played with a smile. If you can't smile, grin. If you can't grin, keep out of the way till you can." With this advice, he showed that even in the most desperate situation, we can uplift, celebrate, and give strength.

When having a conversation, it is helpful to smile. More people will want to talk to you if you are smiling. It is a universal human expression of friendliness and vulnerability that shows you're letting down your guard and reaching out to someone—unless you bare your teeth like a caged tiger, as some are known to do. With a genuine smile, we project openness. It shows we're not hiding anything. Especially in conversation, it means we are enjoying the other's company.

In a good conversation, avoid going into high and low mental states of aggression or depression. Keep a cheerful but genuine touch. Humor is a natural companion, and conversation around a table with friends can be the perfect time to test your wit. Affectionately teasing each other brings levity and light to an exchange. You can make bad puns. Laughing together opens us up and enriches us all.

However, notice when you're using humor aggressively, as a way to hurt others or to avoid true engagement, building a wall with witty replies and sharp words because you're afraid of being touched. In that case, humor is not enriching the conversation. Instead of making a "joke," why not explain that you're not totally comfortable with something that's happening right now, and that you'd like to talk about it?

Humor can be a way to communicate sticky subjects. It may not always be appropriate when situations are dire, but sometimes accessing joy by expressing mirth or silliness can help people come to terms with their dilemma. Poignant medical situations such as palliative care or cancer treatment are often lightened through laughter and humor initiated by patients, which helps the people who are caring for them.

Humor is not just telling jokes; it can be expressed in our demeanor, word choice, or expression. It can often demonstrate our point of view while we stay open and friendly at the same time. Some cultures emphasize humor; others, not so much. With everything there is a balance. If we smile excessively or inappropriately, we may seem foolish. But all cultures share humor, for it is a natural part of life.

Interspersing proverbs, stories, puns, and jokes keeps a conversation lively and engaging. If we're talking about how it is unnecessary to boast about one's intelligence, we might quote the proverb "Serenity is a sign of wisdom." Or if we are experiencing the dramatic fluctuation of March weather, we might say, "In like a lion, out like a lamb." Whether such colloquial bits of wisdom ring true or sound antiquated, they connect us with our collective cultural inheritance and bring it alive in that moment. In the same way, we can tell a joke or recount a funny experience to add color, character, and shape to the conversation.

Like the great Greek plays, our lives and our conversations will always be affected by love, war, tragedy, drama, and comedy. While the general spirit of conversation reflects good windhorse and a positive attitude on life, humor and puns are obviously not always appropriate. They require good timing.

Like children, good conversationalists are always available to participate in the spirit of life. They have the courage to be open, which means their empathy and curiosity toward others can flow. The slogan that applies here is "Always maintain only a joyful mind." Even when someone dies, a good conversationalist is able to be genuinely present, asking a question that invites a grieving person to appreciate the person who has passed: Tell me, how did you meet? When did you first know this was an important person in your life? What do you think she was most proud of? People are social creatures; we need friends the same way we need food and water.

On the other hand, sometimes we become grimmer and tighter, as if we are trying to make ourselves so solid that nothing affects us. We are unavailable. This often only compounds the adversity because we are no longer feeling life's play. Depression seems to be the bottom-line mood. In reality, there is no bottom line as such, for every situation is by nature impermanent. This doesn't mean that a bad situation doesn't feel like an eternity.

It's true that when we're feeling well, we're more likely to smile and joke, but it is just as true that our moods are likely to improve when we show good humor. As expressions of our innate healthiness, smiling and laughing in conversation are simple and effective ways to lighten up on the spot—and it even helps when we're alone. We concede that we should not take ourselves so seriously. This ability to see things from a different perspective is a natural outgrowth of intelligence, for a good dose of humor can help us navigate challenging times.

Reflection

Write down what you feel good about in yourself. Then do it for someone else. For example, you could write that you feel good about your job, your family, or your children, or even your dreams or strengths. What are you good at doing? Consoling people, being gentle, staying focused? Or you could write about what you appreciate about others—their good qualities or accomplishments.

Share Food and Drink

Food, drink, and conversation are not just flourishes to a meaningful life; they're the core elements of every civilization. Food and drink nourish the body, while conversation nourishes the heart and mind. In order to cook the food, there is a sense of warmth. This sparks conversation as well, which promotes communal warmth. By simply enjoying and appreciating these properly, we greatly enrich our lives. They are a natural expression of our dignity.

As in many cultures, for Tibetans, sharing a meal is one of the most important moments of the day and in life. It is a way we can nurture each other. It is not simply about having friends; eating together promotes our health and well-being. In the Tibetan calendar there are feast days that correlate with the lunar cycle. Feasts are about celebrating life, which is centered on food and drink. Food and drink are the result of the harmony between earth, water, fire, and air. Eating and drinking together, we celebrate our interdependence with the elements and one another.

In cultures around the world, tea and coffee provide the basis for social dialogue and conversation. As a stimulant, tea wakes us up. The act of preparing tea itself—the boiling of the water, the steeping of the tea, choosing the china, pouring milk or sugar in the cup—is an excellent topic of conversation because it requires various degrees of precision and engages our senses in the present moment. Through this we open our eyes and see the beauty of the world. This notion of beauty is openness. When we see something beautiful, we are opened.

Many cultures have a tradition of afternoon tea, and in some Asian cultures there is also a midmorning tea. Gathering throughout the day is an ancient method of allowing family and friends to bond. Brewing hot tea creates a genteel atmosphere that soothes everyone. Therefore, sharing a cup of tea is an excellent conduit for having a good conversation.

Sharing a meal or a drink is the most natural way to bond with each other. It creates an atmosphere of trust. The notion of breaking bread indicates peace. Thus the act of eating together generates peace, and the opportunity to connect is a part of that. Granted, meals around the holidays can be challenging because disagreements can flare simply by sitting down together. But by and large, meals are where we gather peacefully.

Whether it's something cool on a hot day or something warm on a cold day, food and drink bring immediate connectivity. Meals can also be very simple or complex, from pizza to elaborate banquets, but that connectivity remains the same. Discussing the food is one of the most natural ways to have conversation. We are sharing our experience. As we eat, a story is created. We often remember great meals by the conversations we have.

For some, a common way to have a conversation is over a drink. Wine, beer, and other intoxicants are an age-old support for conversation. They can relax the mind and body, reducing the level of stress and inciting pleasure. A drink is a mood changer, stimulating the mind and lubricating the tongue, weakening self-consciousness and inhibition. Indeed, alcohol is something of a truth serum, intoxicating us to share things we usually would not. Often we wake up the next morning embarrassed about what we have said and done, so we have more conversations repairing the damage. There is a fine line between relaxing, bonding communally, and digressing into abuse. However, in moderation, drinking allows some of us to express ourselves more clearly in exchange with others.

Having conversation can be so meaningful and potent that it overshadows even questionable food and drink. In fact, we should carefully consider what we eat and drink—and with whom. As the mind-training slogan says, "Abandon poisonous food." If we use conversation for the purpose of building our ego, we are eating poisonous food. The way to abandon it on the spot is to reach out to the other person.

We all work hard to have a home and food, and to be fortunate to have good conversation. When we share them, we are in society at its most primal.

Reflection

If you usually eat alone, invite someone over for tea or a meal, or go out to eat in order to experience the difference between eating alone and eating with others. If you usually eat with others, try eating alone. Reflect on the difference in these experiences.

Everything Can Be Accomplished with Patience

In Chicago, I listened to stories from ex–gang members about trying to stop the violence that had been happening in the city's streets. One way they would do it was to talk with the survivors of shootings, encouraging them not to retaliate. The interrupters told me that their work begins with a simple conversation, and that the process takes months. They have to establish trust, visiting the victims frequently, before even bringing up the topic of what their reactions will be. The road from violence to nonviolence, from anger to forgiveness, can be long and requires great patience.

Being patient is having mastery over oneself and not engaging in aggression. Simply by being willing to be with another person and exchange words, we are developing patience. It is said that patience is the guardian of our good qualities. When we lack patience in conversation, through our aggression we become impatient. Our virtues break down; we become rude and offensive. We are giving in to anger. When we engage in anger, we are hostile to others. We hurt ourselves by damaging previously gained good intentions, and we may hurt the other persons, too. They lose respect for us, and our reputation suffers.

On the other hand, patience does wonders for our standing with others. When we are present in conversation, others think well of us. Patience also makes us more attractive. Our words are more engaging. Our actions have more grace. The sweet perfume of patience attracts everyone. It is a demonstration of internal harmony that allows us to be more accommodating.

Patience is related to good timing and self-discipline in keeping the heart and mind open, and letting go. Being present is key. By focusing on our partner's face—or looking him in the eyes—and coming back to it when we feel distracted, we gain patience. We can also learn patience by letting our partner speak when we most feel like jumping in. We can also practice patience by being willing to let go of what we thought was going to happen. Let the emotions that arise dissolve in the space. Most of all, patience is simply being in the moment, which is always happening, so there's really nowhere else to be.

We all have periods of being more patient and less

patient. When we are healthy and happy, we are more easygoing and accommodating. When misfortune befalls us or we are emotionally challenged, we become tight and impatient, always wanting to move on to the next moment. There are people who test our patience. Some of us may be naturally more patient than others. In conversation, our partner's degree of patience tells us how she is.

As the speed of life increases, as our schedules are more stressed, patience seems less available—and what patience we have is always tested. Yet a few minutes of simple conversation can immediately reconnect us with the benefits of patience. First, because patience is the absence of struggle with ourselves or others, it brings an immediate feeling of harmony and peace. Second, patience tends to repay us in kind. When we are patient with others, they tend to be patient with us.

Within conversation there is patience of body, speech, and mind. In terms of physical patience, perhaps there's something else you'd rather be doing, but instead you're holding your body in the presence of another. Such mastery over your body puts you physically at ease. You can extend that ease by not taking offense if your partner continues to fidget, text, or engage with others in the midst of your conversation. The strength of patience is such that it can accommodate a certain amount of agitation. For inconsiderate people who simply can't interrupt their speedy lifestyle for a conversation, one must decide how far one's patience will extend, and to what benefit. However, if your conversational partner is a child or young adult, their fidgeting is understandable and par for the course. As well, if someone is experiencing pain or discomfort, patience needs to accommodate them.

There is also patience of speech. If others incite us with negative comments, this patience keeps us from immediate retaliation. Instead, we sift through our vocabulary and choose words appropriately, reciprocating with nonaggressive language: "I'll have to contemplate what you just said." Patience of speech also means working with our habitual tendencies, such as excessive flattery or complaint. When you feel you must say something, try listening a bit longer instead. The more patient you are, the less you'll give in to these patterns.

There is also intellectual patience. A conversation may entail hearing philosophical or political views that we don't agree with. When unpleasant or sensitive topics arise in conversation, rather than taking offense or inciting others, we can listen to them. Cultivate beginner's mind. This is a mind of openness, curiosity, and few preconceptions. Knowing that conversation is not about winning a game or suppressing others, we can demonstrate mental mastery by being patient.

If you decide to engage in friendly debate, do so by

employing patience, which is not simply passivism or verbal abstinence. Rather, it is the ability to remain still in your mind, body, and speech. That means choosing not to take offense and not to offend others. Especially in awkward or uncomfortable conversations, intellectual patience shows that our minds are strong against attacks of anger and jealousy. It is the ability to endure.

In ancient India and Greece, conversation, communication, dialogue, and debate happened within the spirit of celebrating the human condition. In Tibetan monastic colleges, debates might center on which virtue is best—knowledge or exertion, patience or generosity. Masters of debate could engage in well-thought-out, synchronized logic and argument while respecting their opponent, maintaining patience, and never digressing into all-out aggression. However, when one is less skilled, what begins as simple conversation can devolve into argument and bickering.

Patience is the natural space needed by both individuals to create their mutual emotional picture. In this way, patience is the accommodator. It is like open sky for two birds flying. If patience were not naturally part of conversation, conversation couldn't manifest. By having patience, people are creating space for each other.

Just by being human, there will always be times when we are offended or, for that matter, offensive.

In this way, an impatient world is a dangerous world. When there are millions of impatient conversations occurring, irritation and rhetoric rise. Instead of peace, there is anger and violence. The great bodhisattva Shantideva says, "A mind that is truly patient does not give rise to anger." The Tibetan word for patience means "forbearance." Forbearance leads to tolerance, which helps us endure hearing opinions with which we don't necessarily agree. Instead, we suffer patiently. To suffer patiently is akin to bravery—the ability to persevere under difficulty.

Whether frustration is building between two individuals or between two nations, by cultivating patience in conversation, we maintain social grace and foster harmony. In the peaceful endeavor of good conversation, we are creating a more stable world.

Reflection

Reflect on a recent conversation that you found annoying or painful. What about the conversation brought this feeling out? This could be the topic of the conversation, the person you were talking to, or the circumstances of your encounter. Looking back, what would you do differently? What qualities could you develop that would make conversations more enjoyable?

Give Bits of Yourself

Generosity in a conversation is the notion of hospitality. When the pace of life was slower, being hospitable in this way was quite natural and feasible. Now, because our age is marked by speed compounded by distractions and short attention spans, we tend to be attached to our time. We may not be such a good host for a conversation because we consider time to be money. To counter this modern outlook, we need to slow down, be generous, and consider conversation to be worthy of our time.

Generosity is the ability to give freely and with warmth, without expecting anything in return. You are offering your mind and heart, caring about and appreciating each other. Focusing in the direction of the other person, you are offering attention. Hearing his stories, challenges, and insights opens you up. When a story touches you, you offer compassion. Hearing about his trials and tribulations, you offer empathy. When he needs encouragement, you cheer him on.

While you are standing or sitting there, engaged in conversation, you are giving your body. Although you could be using it to do other things, you keep your body still in order to converse. Looking at your conversational partner and listening to her words, as you begin to pay more attention, you notice more of her physical expressions. Your attention is becoming finer.

As the conversation continues, you are offering laughter, amusing stories, and details to subtle points. Putting effort into pronouncing and using words properly is also generosity: each word is a jewel you are giving to the other person. Accepting praise graciously is also a gift because it confers pleasure on the person who praised you.

It is said that all gifts we receive in this life are from past acts of generosity, and as the old adage says, "You get what you give." That means that by being generous now, we are laying the ground for good conditions in the future. Our generosity does not disappear; its effects echo through the universe.

On a more practical and immediate plane, generosity in conversation is a two-way street. When you share your time, others tend to share theirs. When you make room in your schedule, others are more accommodating. When you are physically present, others show up, too. When you listen to them, others tend to reciprocate.

In fact, a good conversation is a ceremony of generosity; both people feel enriched and fulfilled, like drinking from the pool of wisdom and connectivity. This exchange of invisible gifts uplifts the mental and physical well-being of both participants, creating a sense of wealth and abundance. Making time for conversation often produces new ideas that begin to shape our world.

Wealth is based on an arbitrary value of what something is worth. Something is "worthless" because the value is no longer relevant. Regarding conversation as an irrelevant social nicety is an alarming indication of how we have devalued human interaction, swinging toward materialism and numbness. Good conversation is a testament to people valuing each other. Without valuing each other, we cannot be generous. Through generosity in conversation, we are creating a new currency based on human worthiness. We are shifting the global tendency from materialism toward humanism, in which our external value system is rooted in internal values.

Without being generous in conversation, it is hard to sit still, relax, and enjoy. Attached to your time, your body, and your schedule—and, most of all, to your habitual patterns—you do not want to include others in your daily plan. Generosity is the ability to be unselfish and nonattached. Attachment generally brings stinginess and anxiety, whereas generosity brings joy and relaxation because we are letting go of our own personal territory.

Prosperity comes from being generous, now and in the future. We attain merit and wisdom by offering physical objects through body; by offering praise, comfort, or inspiring words through speech; and by offering aspiration, fearlessness, and compassion through mind. Giving a physical object, we accumulate merit so that in the future we are physically comfortable. Giving through speech, we accumulate merit so that favorable words occur in the future. Giving through mind, we gain wisdom. All these generous actions are rooted in the view of threefold purity—emptiness of self, action, and other—by which we gain windhorse.

Reflection

To connect with the energy of generosity, offer something from your right hand to your left hand. For example, hold a piece of fruit or a useful object such as a pen or phone. Feel the weight of it and contemplate its qualities. Allow yourself to truly connect with the object as you feel it in one hand. Then extend your other hand, with the palm open, ready to receive. With appreciation, pass the object to the other hand as though offering a gift to another. Feel and appreciate the object and repeat this reflection a few times, passing the object from hand to hand. As you do this, explore the quality of giving, and how this experience can show the way to be more freely giving with others.

Exert Yourself Effortlessly

My father said, "Exertion is not giving up on the hassles of your life." Having exertion in conversation allows us to hang in there with conversations when they are smooth, but it also allows us to stick with conversations that are difficult or arduous.

With exertion, we apply ourselves. This is an aspect of windhorse, which represents success, energy, and accomplishment. Often in the Himalayas, we find the symbol of the horse on flags. Our success, which is represented by the wind, is based on the hard work of the horse. The success comes from application. We apply ourselves by staying curious, by listening, by reciprocating with stories and experience, by asking questions.

We often feel like exertion is a choice. Yet in conversation, as in life, there is moving forward, staying neutral, and moving backward. If we want a conversation to move forward, increasing our connection with and trust in another, then we need to exert ourselves. Nothing will improve while we are being neutral. Moving backward is when negative emotion takes over. Then we find ourselves more belligerent, less kind, and increasingly self-centered. This isn't exertion, because it doesn't lead us toward accomplishment or success.

If we engage only with people we want to be with, or people who agree with us, we find ourselves having only those conversations that are pleasurable or pleasant. Then, when we must stay in a conversation that is challenging, we find that our exertion is underdeveloped and we want to give up. Like a horse that isn't taken out of the stable, we get out of shape.

Exertion is industrious. It counters laziness. Industriousness then leads to auspiciousness. In Tibetan, the word for "auspicious" is *tashi*. It indicates a favorable sign or occurrence that is often spontaneous, or happening suddenly. It is linked to the word for "interdependence," *tendrel*. This implies that when we exert ourselves, we are putting into motion all kinds of unforeseen events.

For example, we may be arguing, and suddenly the wind blows and the door slams shut. Even though this may be a random occurrence, if we have some self-awareness, that sudden noise and jolt might bring us out of our anger and resentment. Or we may not have spent much time with our spouse, so we decide to go for a drive together when suddenly a thundershower breaks, and we see a rainbow. Such auspiciousness in the environment cannot be ignored.

If we apply ourselves in this practice of windhorse, we find more and more auspiciousness happening all the time. That is why the horse is used. The horse is the element of conquering, of acting directly. And like a good conversation, a horse is beautiful, dignified, and cheerful.

The best way to build exertion is to genuinely care for others. As we practice having good conversations, this is what happens. Then exerting ourselves to say the words, listen to another person, and be in a space with them is natural and effortless. This creates joy.

Reflection

Reflect on the pattern of your daily life. In which activities do you really exert yourself? Do you spend more time on social media or watching the news than conversing with family and friends? What do you engage in with gusto? Is there anything in the mix you would like to do differently?

Intelligence Is Your Sword

Conversation can sometimes be a way of engaging in familiar themes that are nonthreatening, comforting, and habitual. Or it can be a way to sharpen your intellect. If you are willing to explore, having conversations can be a way by which to gain insight. The person you're talking to becomes the way to learn more about yourself and your world.

Dropping your own agenda and feeling interest in someone else is like traveling to someone else's country, for each person carries her own culture. Learning about another person in conversation uplifts, intrigues, and invigorates the mind. Your knowledge base increases and you learn more about people in general, increasing your field of experience, with which you can compare and contrast. Your intelligence develops and your insight expands.

In fact, many philosophical and spiritual traditions

can be traced to a single conversation—with a cosmic force, a noble sage, or even with the elements. Many Buddhist sutras are stories of the Buddha's conversations. The *Heart Sutra*, a dialogue between the Buddha and Shariputra, reveals the ultimate intelligence—the absolute wisdom known as *prajna*. The Tibetan translation is *sherap nyingpo,* "the essence of intelligence." The Socratic method of philosophy is also based on asking questions in a very simple approach to knowledge that yields tremendous insight.

In the Shambhala tradition, this inquisitiveness and insight is known as the sword of wisdom, which is depicted by the bodhisattva of wisdom, Manjushri. The sword is surrounded by flames, which represent knowledge and wisdom. The sword is perpetually sharp and can cut through any concepts or illusions.

On a relative level, this notion of wisdom is our own mind. Conversation is a way to access that wisdom. In the humdrum of life, we often ignore what people say. But if we are willing to pay attention to others, a tremendous amount can be learned. Intelligence is the process of how the mind gains knowledge, which is its natural nutrition. It is the ability to compare, contrast, and discern. It leads to insight and good judgment. Just by listening to the words of others as they express themselves can be a profound way of deepening wisdom. In this way, intelligence is applying our minds to the present moment—the here and now.

As you engage in conversation, your intelligence is sharpened. This sharpening process begins with simple curiosity, which stems from your eagerness to learn. Intelligence is the natural grounding factor of conversation. Without intelligence, we would have no way of comprehending one another.

First, we have to determine that the conversation is important, and let go of previous engagements. Then, simply by giving another person our attention, we are focusing the mind. By engaging our sense faculties, we gain tremendous knowledge. Looking at our partner closely gives us an intimate understanding of who he is. Listening to his stories, we gain knowledge about his experience. His emotional expressions offer a taste of his inner life. The subtle nuances of his being transmit human nature.

Some people feel that conversation has nothing to offer. That's because when we have conversation without curiosity, an essential element is missing, and we fail to engage our intelligence. Lack of curiosity is often responsible for a boring or limited conversation.

Pride is often the cause of failure when individuals engage in conversation. Just as stinginess nullifies generosity, pride is the enemy of intelligence. With a mind possessed by pride, we believe there's nothing to be learned, which puts us above simple human communication.

Truly wise individuals are not possessed by haughtiness. They know that even in the most ordinary of activities, there is knowledge to be gained. Many small encounters with ordinary things lead to a greater and greater depth of understanding. Thus throughout history great sages have been depicted having conversations with farmers and children. This demonstrates their compassion and magnanimity but also their intelligence. In every moment, there is something to be learned. Whether the words are simple or complicated, whether the occasion is mundane or extraordinary, knowledge is always available through conversation, the ultimate testament to collective human wisdom. Through conversation, wisdom and knowledge perpetually grow.

Reflection

Reflect on what you have learned in conversations at different times in your life, and from whom. What would you like others to learn from talking to you?

Ordinary Compassion

Compassion is the bonding agent, the ability to be open to the trials and tribulations of another, the simple and profound ability to feel another's pain. Life is fraught with difficulties and challenges that we must navigate. Although both partners may not explicitly express their difficulties, compassion helps them understand that within the human condition, suffering is constant. Compassion in conversation—being available to pain and suffering—can give you the personal fortitude by which to persevere.

Conversely, if you push suffering away, refusing to acknowledge the continual struggle, life becomes narrow and two-dimensional because you are not willing to be open emotionally. You create a cocoon that buffers you from the vast range of human experience. Perhaps you're having trouble handling your own struggle and don't want to listen to someone else's. With compassion, you participate by having empathy and trying to put yourself in another's place. By telling stories, others are describing their experience as accurately as they can. Through this very human exchange of self and other, conversation is powerful as you try to ease another's suffering by saying, "I hope things get better."

Compassion doesn't necessarily have to be dramatic. It is generated naturally—hearing someone else's story expands your heart. Someone could be telling you about having a flat tire on the way to the meeting. By listening to her story, you are sharing that experience. One way to commiserate would be to turn it toward yourself by recounting a similar travail: "I know how you're feeling. It reminds me of losing my luggage flying to my family reunion." Another would be to continue to reaffirm the other's story by staying with it and asking for more details. "Did anyone stop to help you? Did you have a spare? Were you late?" Such simple exchanges about ordinary challenges create a bond because compassion naturally counters self-absorption and ignorance.

A society that is plagued by selfishness lacks compassion. Sometimes we are self-absorbed and listening to our own soundtrack as we walk down the street. We don't notice the homeless person on the street, nor do we care about them. Modern industrial countries need oil, but they only think about their own economy, with little compassion for what we are doing to the environment or the people. In such circumstances, it is difficult to have good communication and conversation. Either we are unaware of others, or we lack the ability to comprehend them.

When we become unsympathetic or isolated like this, each interaction becomes a cold and hard exchange. Individuals are unhappy, society is weak, and everybody suffers. To get back to basics we need to be aware of suffering, foster the feeling of empathy, and care for others. This allows us to open our minds and hearts. You can open your heart just by watching the news and focusing on a particular story that touches you. Being aware of suffering does not make you weak; it makes you realistic. Just to initiate a conversation has a strong element of compassion—there is the hope that an act of simple exchange will help another, or at least be a welcome respite.

As the world becomes more mechanized, human qualities have to be encouraged. Because technology in the form of computers and other digital-age devices replaces human beings, we become used to pushing buttons and getting what we want. People are not buttons. Working with people is like a dance that requires the whole of our being.

The wisdom behind conversation is that by acknowledging each other's humanity through open and communal exchange, we are testifying to the vibrancy of human nature. Compassion gives conversation breadth and scope. It creates a protective netting around the conversation, like a halo that provides a level of comfort and safety in which deep emotional profundity can take place. Like the full moon, compassion gives our conversation a mysterious glow.

Reflection

Think of a time in your life when you were suffering and deserving of compassion. With empathy, imagine water rinsing away the painful memories of regret, self-hatred, and confusion. Extend this feeling of tenderness to include everyone in the present moment who is suffering in the way you suffered in the past. Arouse the intention to open your heart to others.

5

Strive for Conversational Excellence

The Constant Expression of Nowness

Conversation in English or any other modern language usually involves a subject, an object, and a verb. These reveal its natural purpose: communicating with others. Language is a network that fosters a harmonious rapport. By answering the simple question "How are you?" with "I feel fine," language creates a container for our existence. From this, we see the existence of others.

Even offensive language arises within the context of societal expression. Words can determine how we navigate life altogether—whether we are warriors or cowards. Therefore, the more we understand the uses of language and conversation, the more skilled we become at creating the story of ourselves and society at large. Regarding our own and others' words as potent expressions of reality is the very foundation of the sacredness of speech, the conduit for the spirit of life.

When we understand that words are an expression

of nowness, conversation becomes a way to honor life itself. Whether it is subtle or obvious, somewhere within our grammatical stream of expression is an immediate representation of how we regard ourselves and others in that moment. Even though we may have spoken the same words again and again, each time we speak them, we are expressing them in the now. In this way, we could say that in all time and space, there has only ever been one conversation. Past and future conversations are not occurring; there is only the conversation that is happening now.

Real spiritual transmission happens in a very ordinary way, but we have made a concept about what it is. Good conversation transmits the feeling of kindness that comes from an openhearted appreciation of life in all its guises, embodied in the act of listening to ourselves and others now.

Reflection

Identify patterns in your own being that habitually keep you from being present: getting lost in the past or the future, becoming entangled in extreme emotions, constantly being distracted, always putting yourself first, and so on. Make a list of these patterns. Then, each day decide on one pattern to notice. What happens when you're more aware?

Enjoy Language

Conversation is an excellent time to enjoy language. Not only can we enjoy our words' subtlety and profundity, we can experiment with new words and continually improve our vocabulary.

Unless we travel extensively or read ravenously, we tend to have a limited and familiar vocabulary. The average native English speaker is said to have a vocabulary of twenty thousand to thirty-six thousand words. However, being a good conversationalist doesn't always depend on having a big vocabulary. Some well-read and well-traveled people can only engage in lackluster conversation. Others with less exposure and education can carry a conversation with charm and curiosity simply because they appreciate human interaction.

Everyone can enjoy the adventure of trying out a new word or turn of phrase. It all comes down to appreciation. Each word has its own energy, history, and tone. Saying it makes us part of that word's history and culture. For example, the word *virtue* is connected with the word *vir*, meaning "human." The word *sophistication* is connected with *sophist*, meaning "wise."

Often we don't use new words because they intimidate us. We're afraid of sounding distant or arrogant. Clearly, we shouldn't use words to bully others or to boast, but all words have a purpose and a role in expressing the human condition.

If we become intimidated by our own usage of words, our vocabulary and word choice will shrink, handicapping our expressive ability. Instead of exploring new words, we'll use the same word over and over in a variety of ways. Needlessly repeating a word reduces its power. Our limited expression begins to affect the overall quality of our lives; as well, it begins to influence society.

Language reflects society's changes and development. A robust society is marked by a flourishing of the humanities, arts, and sciences—all deeply connected to language and invigorating conversation. When society goes through difficulty, there is a tendency for language to contract. People may simplify their language and express things in a dumbed-down or safe way. As well, each generation separates itself from the previous one by coming up with linguistic differences. Even in the course of one life, we may change our use of language and vocabulary.

Language is related to our level of personal confidence. When we feel bold, we may increase our word choice, and when we feel more vulnerable, we may limit it. If we have a simple relationship to our environment, our word choice may be simple, but if we have an ornate relationship to our environment, our words may be more diverse. Our word choice thus reflects our perception of reality, and the expression of language is intimately connected with our sanity and happiness. When having a conversation, we are using words to weave an invisible web that creates a communal reality.

Reflection

When was the last time you learned a new word? How did you learn it? Consider learning at least one new word daily. Then reinforce your expanding vocabulary by using these words in conversation frequently.

Love Is an Awesome Power

As we engage in conversation, we hear about another person's hopes and dreams, and a simple yet powerful love occurs. This may not be a romantic love, but love in a more basic sense: the ability to delight in the welfare of others. We care. We want things to go well for them. Love is the power of wishing someone well.

Love is an awesome power that can drive an individual as well as a society. It is a unique combination of emotional sensitivity and resilience that is demonstrated clearly by parents' love for their children, as well as citizens' love for their nation. Even in these very confusing times, when the themes of patriotism and loyalty are trigger points for intense emotions and fear, there is still a basic wish to find pride and foster affection for our own culture. Appreciating culture is part of human nature. Before competitiveness or hatred arises, when we might think our country is better than others, we all feel a simple appreciation for our own culture.

As an emotion and an experience, love can be so raw that it is easily misunderstood. However, in its pure form, love is not extreme; if it were, it could not sustain itself. Although it can appear misguided or foolish, love has the power to give life.

For a meaningful human life, we yearn for the thread of love within. A conversation demonstrates this yearning for connection—wanting to love and to be loved. Even simple conversation can be an expression of deep altruism that wants to share and celebrate with another.

We all need love and encouragement. We need to feel it personally, and we need to be able to express it to others as well. In this way, conversation has bilateral benefits: to be able to give love is one of the most potent rewards in life, and being able to receive love is one of life's greatest treasures. Love may not seem to be in the air at times, but it lies within the undercurrent of every conversation.

Anger, jealousy, and other socially abrasive emotions can be the result of a complicated story line of how love was not felt. We might be numb and rude because we feel unloved. It takes a long time for such wounds to heal, but through conversing and exchanging with others, we can begin to feel love again.

Even though love is always being manipulated and commercialized by advertising and our entertainment culture, the energy of love remains resilient and pure in conversations between parents and children, friends and loved ones, and even between employers and employees. Conversation is the tip of the communal iceberg. This is a fitting analogy because in our modern world, we often feel frozen in the ability to express love and affection. Engaging in conversation creates warmth; as we warm up to each other, love naturally ensues. In this way, love is only a simple conversation away.

On the other hand, even if you love someone dearly, it is said that a medium level of love is ideal because then it's sustainable. In the same way, in social interactions we can have affection for one another, but we don't need to always be talking about it. There is a social medium, which is kindness. If we deploy kindness in everyday action, we can sustain it. In its pure form, conversation is two individuals engaging in kindness—giving time, energy, and space to each other in a conversation. It is a sustainable form of affection, love, and appreciation. By lending our ears, exchanging thoughts and pleasantries, a simple level of kindness is taking place. In relationships, we cannot say, "I love you" all day long. But by talking about how another person is doing, having tea, having dinner, or going for a walk, we can sustain the feeling of kindness.

Reflection

In a short meditation, bring someone you love to mind and say the words "I want you to be happy." How does this feel? Now try it with someone toward whom you feel neutral, then someone you don't like at all, even an enemy. Does the wish feel different according to whom you're wishing it for? Can you generate the wish for all beings to be happy?

The Ultimate Conversation

Finally, what makes good conversation great is wisdom—the wisdom to see your world. Wisdom understands that the premise of the conversation is much broader in scope than the simple give-and-take of words. It understands that conversation doesn't necessarily need a point. It recognizes that through having conversation, humanity is always feeling its own worth, within which is wisdom itself.

Unlike knowledge, wisdom doesn't need to be learned; it is inherent. Inherently, humans understand that contact and exchange is good, and therefore that humanity is good. Engaging in conversation demonstrates our trust in that goodness. We know that conversation is not a waste of time. As we connect in the moment, we are the inheritors of human wisdom throughout the ages, which is respect for others and society. We are laying the foundations for the future of society and humanity as a whole.

Through this awareness, conversation becomes the conduit for wisdom to flow, and wisdom is the ultimate unspoken space through which the spoken words of the conversation are expressed. This is how wisdom aligns us with our own inherent goodness, and ultimately allows society to recognize its own goodness.

Wisdom—that which never needs to be expressed—allows for conversation to occur. Before they are expressed, words—and the concepts and ideas behind those words—are formulated from wisdom. Afterward, they dissolve back into wisdom. One can see words as expressions of wisdom, and wisdom as the element of the inexpressible in each word. Without wisdom, words could not even be formed; without wisdom, words would be meaningless. At the same time, ultimately their meaning is beyond words, and therefore beyond themselves. Words are like wisdom expressing wisdom to itself.

We can see this truth at work when we repeat any word again and again. At some point it becomes meaningless. The shell of that word is stripped down; all that remains is its un-wordness. Thus we are left simply with our own minds. This leads us to wisdom. That's how we discover that ultimately no word is satisfactory, not even *happiness* or *joy*. The only thing that is truly satisfactory is wisdom. Wisdom is that which is free from ignorance. It is the state of cognizance, or pure knowing. This wisdom is said to be the inherent nature of our own minds. At a primordial level, we know that we are free of ignorance. Here, instead of dwelling in a perpetual state of not knowing, we simply know. When we come to this deep understanding, we realize that thoughts are a pure expression of this wisdom. Then, when we speak, the words we utter come from a place of knowing.

In this way, language is simply our wish to connect with that inherent wisdom inside us, which is embedded in every language. In this way, in deep spiritual traditions, ultimately all sounds are considered to be expressions of wisdom. Language is not a method of confining us, but a way to express who we are.

Language is a constant barrage of sounds that are perpetually trying to paint the picture of wisdom, which ultimately cannot be done. However, if we see these words simply as the natural expression of wisdom—wisdom's attempt to show us our inherent wisdom—then all words can become an expression and transmission of wisdom.

In this light, there are no good words and no bad words. All words are equal. They are like mantras, with the ability to transmit something beyond their own utterance. Each word contains the construct of humanity trying to understand and express itself. Therefore, all conversations are a proclamation of human wisdom. This is the never-ending conversation that is always occurring. Thus, as we engage in conversation, we are joining this cosmic conversation, which is beginning-less, and will be endless.

Reflection

Sit in silence with a friend for a few minutes or more. Don't speak, rest together, and see what is communicated beyond words. Gaze into each other's eyes, smile, and enjoy the simple truth of being in the company of another. When it feels right, talk and be together as two good human beings on this earth.

Final Note: Host a Salon

Historically, a place where the art of conversation thrived was the salon. Usually associated with seventeenth- and eighteenth-century French literary and philosophical movements, salons took place in urban settings until as recently as the 1940s. Grounded in respect for the inherent power of communication, these small gatherings were often hosted and moderated by women, who would also choose the topic of conversation. As simple as salons appeared, they had a profound effect on the evolving societies around them.

Salons are still an excellent way to engage in the art of conversation, and to some degree we have revived the tradition with our book clubs and study groups. A twenty-first-century salon can be a dinner party or a small gathering in someone's living room. One may choose a theme for conversation, such as a book we've all read, or simply let the group mind flow where it may. The basic criterion is that the participants have respect for one another and listen with intention. As well, in order to have good dialogue and conversation, everyone must have ample time to speak and listen. These gatherings provide an opportunity to bond, to express themes and ideas, and to have dialogue.

Especially in this day and age, when the threat of hatred and polarization among us seems to be so strong, I encourage you to host or participate in a conversation group. Through salons, the art of good conversation can become the method by which we work to shift our current story of isolation and numbness to one of curiosity and participation.

There are lots of ways to do this. Build a group around a theme that interests everyone—aging or parenting, for example—and agree to discuss it at a monthly brunch. Or start a group with the notion of discussing difficult questions that you might actually all disagree on. Invite a different combination of people in for conversation and refreshments one day a week after work. Take turns hosting and choosing the theme. The point isn't to convince each other, but to show interest in others and build community even when we hold different points of view. It's an opportunity for everyone to be heard.

Or consider visiting a Shambhala Center, where

you will usually find a weekly gathering that includes food, meditation, and conversation. For many years, I've been presenting the notion of society as really just two human beings communicating. At a personal, familial, and community level, this can manifest simply as the three things we're celebrating—food, conversation, and meditation. I certainly hope you are able to participate in these foundational elements of an enlightened society: the enjoyment of nutritious food as we connect with one another through conversation, and the strengthening of our minds through meditation practice. To find a Shambhala Center near you, visit www.shambhala.org.

Acknowledgments

First and foremost, I would like to thank my father, the first Sakyong, the Dorje Dradül of Mukpo, Chögyam Trungpa Rinpoche, who demonstrated true warriorship and taught me about the importance of good conversation. I would like to thank my wife, the Sakyong Wangmo, Dechen Chöying Sangmo, for showing me how to completely enjoy life and all my relationships through conversation.

As ever, thank you to my illustrious editor, Emily Hilburn Sell, who continually amazes me with her patience and skill.

Thank you to the Shambhala teachers who generously and enthusiastically contributed tips and exercises for the book. Thanks to Mark Whaley for always showing up, and to James Milani for his diligence and care. Thanks to Alicia Symchych and Carolyn

Krusinski for their stalwart clear-sightedness, research, and support on this project and many others.

As ever, thank you to my agent, Reid Boates, for his enthusiasm about my work. Thank you to my editor at Penguin Random House, Gary Jansen, and all the other good helpers at Harmony.

About the Author

Sakyong Mipham is the head of Shambhala, a global network of meditation and retreat centers. The Shambhala tradition emphasizes confidence in the enlightened nature of all beings and teaches a courageous life based on wisdom and compassion in order to build enlightened society. The Sakyong—literally "earth protector"—also holds the Kagyü and Nyingma lineages of Tibetan Buddhism. As part of the Mukpo clan of eastern Tibet, he is descended from the Tibetan warrior-king Gesar of Ling.

Sakyong Mipham is the author of *Turning the Mind into an Ally, Ruling Your World, Running with the Mind of Meditation,* and *The Shambhala Principle.* He is also an avid poet, artist, and athlete. Through the Sakyong Foundation, he engages in supporting organizations and projects whose activities exemplify the vision of Shambhala. He travels extensively, teaching throughout the world.

For more information, see sakyong.com.